The State of Florida
Community Association Manager (CAM)
License Examination

Complete Study Guide

First Edition 2019

The State of Florida
Community Association Manager (CAM)
License Examination

Complete Study Guide
First Edition 2019

Published by:
Kindle Digital Publishing (KDP)

Author:
Ray Fernandez

Edition:
First Edition, Fall 2019

Copyright © 2019. All Rights Reserved

Table of Contents

Introduction
Using This Book
Preparing for the CAM Examination
Florida CAM Licensing Requirements
Inside the Test - A look at the State CAM Exam
Fundamentals of Association Management
Exam Prep Core Material
    Part I - Law
    Part II - Procedures
    Part III - Budgets/Finance
    Part IV - Insurance
    Part V - Management & Maintenance
Test Topics - Full Outline
Exam Prep Questions
Legal References and Statutes
Final Checklist Before Taking the Exam
Glossary
Index
References

Introduction

Community associations are private, non-profit organizations which are comprised of members and residents of the local community. They hold meetings, vote to fill board positions, and prepare an annual budget, amongst other activities. Most residential homeowners associations in Florida are established as entities in which membership is a condition of ownership of a unit, or lot, townhouse, villa, condominium, and so forth - and the association is authorized to impose a fee on the unit, which can one day may become a lien on the parcel.

As a safeguard to protect the general consumer, laws and regulations have been enacted to establish boundaries of authority and obligations of the association, and obligations for the managers to obtain proper licensing and credentials as well.

Community Association Managers (CAMs) are those persons or firms, who actively operate and administer resident associations, such as condos and HOAs. A special state license is not required to become a member of a homeowners association, to be on the Board, or even to sit as its President. However, it *is* a requirement if you plan to perform community management *as a profession*.

This publication is provided as a study guide and reference manual for candidates preparing to embark on that journey and take the State of Florida Community Association Manager (CAM) license examination. Community association "management" refers to the physical operation and execution of the local homeowners association duties and tasks, and this is typically performed by what is known as a "CAM firm".

The CAM examination is a computer-based test administered by the State that will certify your knowledge of state and federal laws pertaining to the operation and management of community associations, preparation of community association budgets, procedures for noticing and conducting community association meetings, insurance matters relating to community associations, management skills, and association maintenance.

The Florida Community Association Manager license is a requirement for those professionals, consultants, advisors and other contracted entities who engage in the paid practice of running condominium, cooperative or homeowner associations. Most states have some form of CAM licensure, and it has become the de facto industry standard license for persons, or firms, who wish to engage the public actively and do business as community association managers.

The learning material and laws presented here are specific to the State of Florida, and is not intended for use with other states, however much of the concepts are the same, and the general basis for having community association licensing is the same. This guidebook provides a concise and effective reference tool, with summaries of the topics covered in the exam, and is an ideal aid in preparation for taking the state test.

This study guide is intended to be used as a reference guide and preparatory tool for candidates preparing to take the State of Florida's Community Association Manager liccnse examination. It is not intended for use with other states, but much of the concepts are the same, and the general basis for having community association licensing is the same. This study guide provides a concise and effective reference tool, with summaries of the topics covered in the exam, and is an ideal aid in preparation for taking the state test.

Keep this reference manual handy, and in particular once you have taken in all the major concepts, refer to the *"Test Topics - Full Outline"* section in the days before the test, and be sure that you have a comfortable familiarity with all those listed knowledge points. The examination consists of 100 multiple choice questions based on entry-level knowledge of the subject, but the information can be challenging. We have provided this study guide to help you navigate your way to the CAM license.

Using This Book

This Study Guide will outline the necessary concepts you need to know in order to pass the examination. The test is not impossible, it is moderately challenging- and it will sufficiently test you on the knowledge and familiarity of these concepts. The goal of this textbook is to introduce these knowledge points to you in an organized fashion which is designed specifically to, and formatted in alignment with, the State-mandated curriculum for the CAM test. There is a specific learning path and personal requirements to become a CAM, most importantly, you must take the required Pre-Licensure learning class, which is available online or in-person.

THIS STUDY GUIDE IS NOT A SUBSTITUTE FOR THE REQUIRED PRE-LICENSURE LEARNING REQUIREMENTS The pre-licensure education requirement consists of an 18-Hour Course that must be delivered by an authorized education provider.

You will need the completion certificate from the course provider before you become eligible to take the test. Don't worry if this sounds like a complicated process, it's not. And best of all, you have this book to help you navigate that application process, so we will try to make it easier for you!

Please refer to the chapter, "*Getting Ready to Take the Exam*", where we explore the application process and what you need to know in the time leading up to the state examination.

Per the Florida Department of Business and Professional Regulation (DBPR) guidelines, only licensed providers who have been authorized to provide the pre-licensure educational course are permitted to deliver classroom or online training in order to satisfy the learning requirements for the license. It is not permissible to simply train for the test and sit for the state exam. In order to become authorized for enrollment at the electronic testing center, you will have to submit the proof-of-completion for your pre-licensure course.

Don't worry, as it is easy to find a great CAM school. You can find several of these providers listed online, and many of them have classroom learning options, available in most major cities. You may have to travel a county or two over, in order to get in on a great class.

More and more students are opting for the online learning route, as it can be faster and more affordable to do so. For those who really yearn for the classroom experience, and like the delivery format of live instructional speech, then please enroll in the in-person class. Online-only learning takes a certain extra dedication, as you have to self-deliver the bulk of the learning materials directly to yourself.

To emphasize further, this is not the official course textbook from one of the pre-licensure course providers. This is a generalized Study Aid for the upcoming state examination. The author is not specifically affiliated with one certain provider or another. We encourage you to research all the available CAM schools and make the selection that is most appropriate for you.

Helpful Tip

The Florida DBPR website provides a list of the approved Pre-Licensure learning providers, where you can research schools and make a choice from there based on your preferences.

This supplemental learning guide is ideally suited for reading during, or after, your pre-licensure course progress. It is recommended to take the standard course first, available from the pre-approved education providers authorized by the State of Florida, before moving on to supplemental learning aids such as flash cards, sample test questions, or cram-sheets. This book is intended to be a supplemental reference tool only, and not a substitute for the required learning path.

Preparing for the CAM Exam

First of all, congratulations on your decision to become a Community Association Manager, and best of luck to you as you prepare to take the final steps towards certification!

Perhaps you are taking the Pre-Licensure course now, or have just recently completed it. Next, you are getting ready to face the state examination and you need a clear, concise textbook delivery of the educational topics in a way that is designed to help you prepare for the test itself. During your pre-licensure course you may have been presented with a straightforward A-to-Z approach to the learning materials, but now that you may have been introduced to the topics and have a fundamental understanding of the core concepts, ultimately the best approach as you near testing would be to align your learning path in a way that is in tune with the design of the test.

Thankfully, Florida DBPR annually discloses the distribution of these topics. As you look over the test topics, you will see how the distribution of the test questions focus on some topics more than others. As a result, the author has structured the learning material to be aligned in-step with the required learning curriculum.

This study guide will prepare you for the Community Association Manager examination by covering the essential elements of the curriculum with a focus on the particular sections of material wherein more attention is emphasized on the examination. This text is organized in alignment with the specific topic areas required for the state test.

Helpful Tip

In the state examination, half of the test questions are based on content from two of the five main parts. These are the "Procedures" and "Budgets" sections. Be sure to know those well and be very familiar with the content, as it's 50% of the exam!

This supplemental learning guide is ideally suited for reading during, or after, your pre-licensure course progress. It is recommended to take the standard course first, available from the pre-approved education providers authorized by the State of Florida, before moving on to supplemental learning aids such as flash cards, sample test questions, or cram-sheets. This book is intended to be a supplemental reference tool only, and not a substitute for the required learning path.

The Florida CAM test consists of **100 multiple-choice questions** based on entry-level knowledge of community association management activities, laws, and practices.

The examination covers these 5 main knowledge areas:

LAW - In the "Law" section, the focus is on State and Federal laws relating to the operation of all types of community associations, governing documents, and state laws relating to corporations and nonprofit corporations . The hierarchy of how these laws inter-relate to each other and how to determine the proper outcome is explored.

PROCEDURES - The "Procedures" part of the material focuses on the physical process for providing notice, and conducting community association meetings. Throughout this textbook and often used in the parlance of association managers, the activities surrounding the process of providing the advance notification of meetings and voting topics, is known as "noticing". Please be cognizant of this distinction as it departs from the normal use of the word.

BUDGETS - In the "Budgets" section we explore the process for the preparation of community association budgets, and related community association finance activities. The core funding component that provides the means for running the association are assessments, which are levied upon the members. Therefore the handling and practice of identifying and organizing the assessment process is critical to a smooth running association.

INSURANCE - This section explores several Insurance matters and how they relate to Community Associations, such as Liability insurance, Worker's Comp, D&O and other types of insurance. There are many cases in which the homeowners association will solicit and engage with an insurance provider to obtain a specific type of coverage.

MANAGEMENT - In the "Maintenance" section, we explore how association management boards deal with maintenance issues. There are some specific requirements, especially regarding Pools and Elevators, that community associations need to be aware of.

Helpful Tip

After reading this textbook and completing the required Pre-Licensure 18-Hour Course, refer to the final section of this book, "*Getting Ready to Take the Exam*", for a step-by-step Licensing Checklist to help you along the way to getting the license.

In addition, the section "*Test Topics-Full Outline*" provides a direct list of the specific examination topics outlined for your convenience.

Licensing Requirements

The specific Florida CAM Licensing requirements are discussed here. Familiarize yourself with all the required elements in advance, so you know what's coming as you navigate the application process and ultimately, schedule an appointment for the state exam. After you have completed the application requirements, which includes steps such as submitting fingerprinting, background checks, and the educational component, you are then ready to schedule the state examination at the Pearson Vue testing center. Completion of the pre-licensure course requires the successful completion of the course test, think of this as a precursor to the main test.

The CAM test is administered via an electronic testing system, and will take place at the testing provider's location. The entire testing process is done via computer system. Candidates input their responses to the multiple-choice questions by entering the answer of their choice.

Each year, the Florida Department of Professional and Business Regulation (DBPR) publishes the Candidate Information Booklet (C.I.B.), which outlines those specific items and will include any newly-added requirements which may have been incorporated after the date of this publication.

Helpful Tip

After you have completed the required Pre-Licensure 18-Hour Course, refer to the final section of this book, "Getting Ready to Take the Exam", for a step-by-step Licensing Checklist to help you along the way to getting the license.

The Department of Business and Professional Regulation has retained the services of Pearson VUE to schedule, administer, score and report the results for computer based testing. Pearson VUE is a leading provider of assessment services to regulatory agencies and national associations and offers licensing and credentialing support services to associations, state agencies, and private industry. After completing the Pre-Licensing education and other required items for the application, you will take the state examination at a Pearson VUE location.

Requirements to Become a Community Association Manager

These are the specific requirements (for Florida), to be able to sit for and take the state examination and become a CAM:

- Candidate must be at least 18 years of age.
- Candidate must first receive approval of the state application, before scheduling the computer-based test. This involves a fingerprint/background check, fees, and other requirements.
- The candidate must successfully complete a state approved 18-hour course, from a licensed provider. The course completion certificate is submitted to DBPR as part of the application process.
- Successfully pass the 100-Question state examination at the Pearson VUE testing center.
- It is not a requirement to be a Florida resident, you can live in another state. However, the candidate may have to travel to Florida to sit for the state examination at the Testing Provider's location.

After you have completed the application requirements (fingerprinting, background check) and the educational component (pre-licensure course and successful completion of the course test), you are then ready to schedule the state examination at the Pearson Vue testing center.

Inside the Test- A look at the State CAM Exam

The Community Association Manager examination is computer-based, and consists of **100 multiple-choice questions** based on entry level knowledge of state and federal laws pertaining to the operation and management of community associations, preparation of community association budgets, procedures for noticing and conducting community association meetings, insurance matters relating to community associations, management skills, and association maintenance.

The Florida Department of Business and Professional Regulation (DBPR) has retained the services of Pearson VUE to schedule, administer, score and report the results for computer based testing. Pearson VUE is a leading provider of assessment services to regulatory agencies and national associations and offers licensing and credentialing support services to associations, state agencies, and private industry. The CAM test is administered using a multiple-choice, computer-based testing system.

Helpful Tip

Once you have completed the required Pre-Licensure education (18-Hour Course), and other required items in the application process such as Fingerprints and Background Check, you will then schedule a testing appointment at a Pearson VUE location to sit for your Florida CAM test.

To save time, you can start the online application with Florida DBPR first, and then embark on the other application steps afterwards.

Breakdown of Exam Topics

The CAM license examination covers the following subject matter, and also shown here is the percentage of test questions that will come from each section. For example, you can see that half of all the questions are centered around two topic areas, BUDGETS and PROCEDURES. Be sure to know those sections well. INSURANCE is the least-covered topic area, with only 12% of the questions based on that section.

LAW (20%)

The LAW section covers an overview of State and Federal laws relating to the operation of all types of community associations, governing documents, and state laws relating to corporations and nonprofit corporations. Also covered in this section is the hierarchy of laws and how they relate to each other, and which ones can supersede others.

PROCEDURES (25%)

In the PROCEDURES section, the actual mechanics of how to run a community association are explored. This part focuses on the procedure for noticing (providing advanced notice of upcoming meetings) and conducting community association meeting sessions, and certain rules related to how those are to be carried out.

BUDGETS (25%)

In the BUDGETS section we explore the preparation of community association budgets, the ratification process of budget approval, how assessments are calculated, and other community association finance topics.

INSURANCE (12%)

The INSURANCE section covers insurance matters relating to Community Associations, such as Liability and D&O insurance. Insurance guidelines for both the property owner and unit owner are examined in this section.

MANAGEMENT (18%)

This section explores topics relating to association management and maintenance, such as the bidding and contracting process, and pool and elevator maintenance guidelines.

The state examination will contain questions from the five main knowledge areas: Law, Budgets, Procedures, Insurance, and Maintenance.

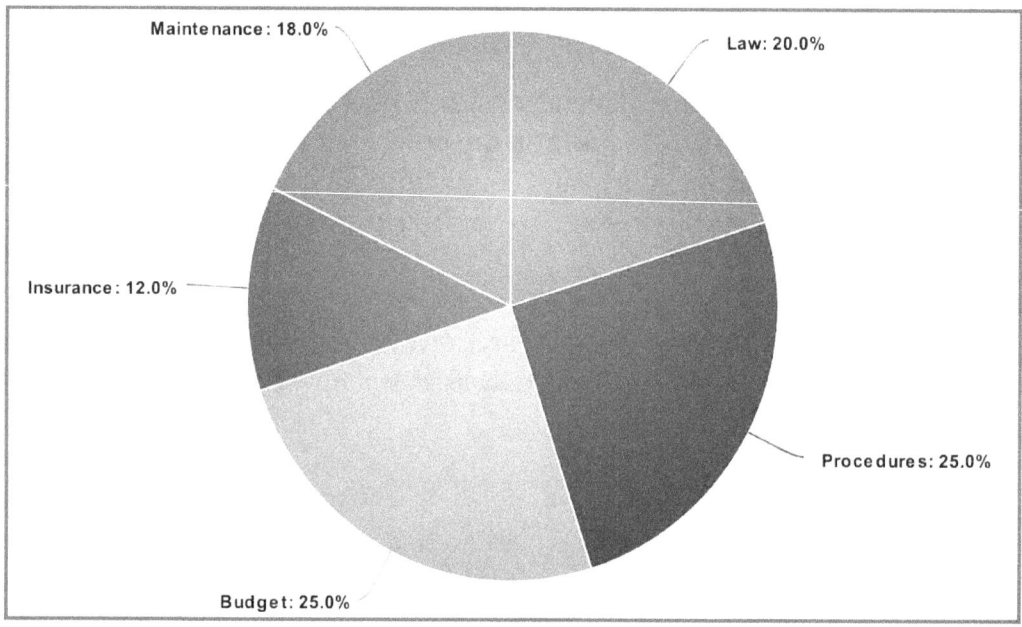

Diagram (Distribution of Exam Questions) - The diagram above illustrates the distribution of test questions for each of the 5 knowledge areas. Notice that half of the examination is centered around 2 of them, **Budget** and **Procedures**. It's important to know those two sections very well to be comfortably prepared to take the test.

Fundamentals of Association Management

Today, most construction of new residential housing is taking place in communities in which there is an association, such as a Homeowners Association (HOA), or a Condominium Association (CO). They are everywhere, and quickly becoming the norm. Together we will explore what they are and how they operate.

"Community association" is defined as a residential homeowners' association in which membership is a condition of ownership of a unit in a planned unit development, or of a lot for a home or a mobile home, or of a townhouse, villa, condominium, cooperative, or other residential unit which is part of a residential development scheme and which is authorized to impose a fee which may become a lien on the parcel.

For a majority of the recent years, there has been a growing number of community associations being formed in the state of Florida. In most cases, these are in newly-developed neighborhoods and condominiums, although an established community can opt to form a homeowner's association in situations where there might not have been one prior. Or, for legal purposes or other intentions, the organizational entity itself may have evolved, such as a condominium later becoming a cooperative later in its lifecycle.

This chapter will explore the fundamental concepts of community association management, how they are organized and used today, and how proper management is required to maintain a stable and productive homeowner's association. Here you will find a basic understanding of the need and purpose of community associations, how they operate, and some of the legal requirements involved. We also review some concepts as it relates to becoming a community association manager as your career choice.

Introduction to Community Association Management

The fundamental principle is, a community association is a non-profit, private organization that is made up of members of the community. Whether its a condominium, subdivision, or cooperative, these organizations are known collectively as "community associations". These entities are private members-only organizations, usually chartered as Non-Profit corporations, whose membership is comprised of members (residents) of the community who automatically become enrolled once they have purchased property in that location.

A community association is a residential homeowners' association in which membership is a condition of ownership of a unit in a planned unit development, or of a lot for a home or a mobile home, or of a townhouse, villa, condominium, cooperative, or other residential unit which is part of a residential development scheme and which is authorized to impose a fee which may become a lien on the parcel.

In most cases the resident automatically becomes a member of the association as soon as they have closed and acquired the property in that community. As a member of the association, the property owner is eligible to vote and participate in association matters. There is an annual meeting that is open for all to attend, and these are usually larger and longer meetings in which more voting activity takes place. Association members are also encouraged to attend and view the smaller monthly or quarterly board meetings as well.

The community association is the entity that is responsible for the management and upkeep of the common areas, and membership in that association is usually a condition of purchasing a home in that community. Meaning that, by becoming a property owner in that community, they are also automatically becoming a member in the association. The association is funded by assessments which are levied against the individual property owners, and these funds are used for the management and maintenance of the property. Because of the sensitive nature of the budgeting process and levying charges against its members, the voting process is a highly-scrutinized affair and ample notice must be given to all voting parties to ensure that the have been provided with sufficient time to study the issues at hand.

Community Association Managers are often confused for Property Managers, so let's take a moment to examine the fundamental differences. The role of the property manager is typically associated with collecting rents, performing repairs, placing tenants into apartment units, and other "landlord" functions. Property Managers are usually managing single-family or multi-family properties, such as apartments or duplexes.

The community association manager is an administrator of condominiums and homeowners associations, at its most basic core definition. The community manager deals primarily with *owners of properties*, as opposed to property managers who deal with *renters of properties*. At the helm of most condominiums, cooperatives, and larger homeowners associations, you will find a CAM hard at work!

The community association manager, or management firm, handles the daily operations and processes for running the homeowners association. Most recently the trend has formed where there are essentially two types of community association managers, the "onsite" manager and the "portfolio" manager. The onsite manager is usually in charge of a single property, and is often a resident of the community. The portfolio manager, in contrast, is responsible for the administration of multiple associations, and thus is usually not a resident of the community. It is easy to see how the community association manager is often confused for the property manager though, as the two do have some parallel duties which are very similar. For example, they both collect assessments, prepare reports, manage disputes, and negotiate and select contractors.

Now, let's take a look at the basic functions of a community association. When an owner buys a home in a subdivision (aka planned community, CDD, etc), they are automatically granted membership in the community's local homeowners association. It is not a requirement of the homeowner to attend all the meetings or participate actively, as some choose to do exactly that. This is certainly not recommended because the owner could miss out on critical information or items to vote on.

Conversely, the interested homeowner who wishes to participate more extensively in the affairs of the community and the maintenance of the common areas can opt to become a member of the Board, Volunteer, Committee Member, or even the President. All homeowners in the community are encouraged to participate and play an active role in the management of the community.

These are the main concepts to keep in mind:

- The community association, in most cases a Condominium or Homeowners Association (HOA), is the entity that is responsible for the management and upkeep of the common areas, handling contractors and maintenance providers, and ensuring the physical appearance of the community via the enforcement of restrictions.

- Membership in that association is usually a condition of purchasing a home in that community. Therefore, by becoming a property owner in that community, they are also automatically becoming a member in the association.

- The association is funded by assessments which are levied against the individual property owners, and these funds are used for the management and maintenance of the property.

- Because of the sensitive nature of the budgeting process and levying charges against its members, the voting process is a highly-scrutinized affair and ample notice must be given to all voting parties to ensure that the have been provided with sufficient time to study the issues at hand.

- The essential purpose of regulating community association managers is to ensure that the proper and ethical procedures are being followed at all times, and that all members are being provided with a fair chance to vote or be heard.

Community Association Management as a career

The proliferation of community associations has grown significantly in the past few decades. Just in the state of Florida, there are nearly fifty-thousand community associations, with about 8 million people residing in them. Almost one-fifth of the entire nation lives in community associations, while the value of those homes located in these community associations is almost five trillion dollars!

About 70% of community associations are managed by professional community association managers or management companies. There is a growing need for licensed and certified CAMs in Florida. At the time of this writing, there are approximately 8,000 community association management firms and around 100,000 individuals employed by management companies in the state.

Now that you have made the decision to pursue a career in community association management, it's important to arm yourself with the tools needed for success. The first step in this career path is to successfully navigate and pass the state exam, and for this you will need an accurate and resourceful study guide!

This study guide aims to prepare you for the Community Association Manager examination by covering the essential elements of the curriculum with a focus on the particular sections of material wherein more attention is emphasized on the examination.

Exam Prep Core Material

The Florida CAM examination will test your knowledge of state and federal laws pertaining to the operation and management of community associations, preparation of community association budgets, procedures for conducting notices and community association meetings, insurance matters relating to community associations, management skills, and association maintenance. It is intended to be entry-level in nature, but it still can be challenging material. It is the design of this study guide to logically present to the reader the essential elements of the curriculum with a focus on the particular sections of material wherein more attention is emphasized on the examination.

The five main parts, or knowledge areas, to be familiar with for the state examination are **Law, Procedures, Budgets/Finance, Insurance**, and **Maintenance** topics.

Make sure you are comfortable with the fundamental concepts of each section, and know the key laws by name and their purpose, for example - for business or legal matters related to Homeowners Associations (HOAs), then you must know that those guidelines and laws are outlined in Florida Statutes Chapter 720, known as the Homeowners Association Act.

Don't worry, you won't have to memorize a bunch of mundane laws! The ones you need to know for the test are actually not that hard to memorize, and they are presented to you here in this text in a straightforward, logical order to facilitate easy recognition and recall.

Below is the list of the topic areas, and the percentage of test questions that will come from each section. For example, you can see that half of all the questions are centered around two topic areas, BUDGETS and PROCEDURES. Be sure to know those sections well. INSURANCE is the least-covered topic area, with only 12% of the questions based on that section.

The five knowledge areas upon which the test questions are based:

PART I (20%)	**LAW**
PART II (25%)	**PROCEDURES**
PART III (25%)	**BUDGETS**
PART IV (12%)	**INSURANCE**
PART V (18%)	**MANAGEMENT**

To prepare best for the examination, ensure that you are competently familiar with the main testing topics and the content covered in each one. Reread each section as needed to become thoroughly familiar with the information. Notice how the "Budgets" and "Procedures" sections are the areas with the most exposure.

Helpful Tip

In the state examination, half of the test questions are based on content from two of the five main parts. These are the "Procedures" and "Budgets" sections. Be sure to know those well and be very familiar with the content, as it's 50% of the exam!

Part I - Law (20%)

In this section we will explore the various laws that affect community associations and the physical management of community associations. As a safeguard to protect the general consumer, laws and regulations have been enacted to establish boundaries of authority and obligations of the association, and obligations for the managers to obtain proper licensing and credentials as well.

These laws were established before the professional practice of community association management as a licensed career developed and grew. They exist to govern and outline the procedures for community associations to follow, regardless of whether they have contracted a professional CAM to perform management duties or not.

The Florida Statutes stipulate that:

- The manager shall not knowingly misrepresent facts, shall undertake to perform only those community management services which they can reasonably expect to complete with professional competence, shall exercise due professional care in the performance of community association management services, and shall not permit others to carry out on his or her behalf, either with or without compensation, acts which, if carried out by the licensee or registrant would place him in violation of Florida Statutes.
- A licensee or registrant shall be deemed responsible by the division for the actions of all persons who perform community association management related functions under their supervision and direction.

Legislation that affects community management varies from Federal to State, to even the local levels. Understand that there is a hierarchy to the laws, in the event of conflicting guidance or overlapping scope. In most cases, Federal law has the highest authority, and in disputed matters this might supercede lower level legislation.

This section covers 20% of the test material, so be sure to familiarize yourself well with this material. Most of the learning material and laws presented here are specific to the State of Florida, and is not intended for use with other states, however much of the concepts are the same, and the general basis for having community association licensing and regulation is the same. Basically, it exists to protect the people from harm or property value loss as a result of improper association practices.

The specific topics covered in the examination are detailed below, as part of the general learning outline for this section. These are the required concepts and knowledge areas to study and be well-familiar with in your preparation for the state exam.

This is the first part, of the five main parts of the textbook, that will explain these topics and prepare you with a fundamental understanding of these laws and legal concepts.

EXAM TOPICS FOR PART I - LAW

1. Utilize the Not-for-Profit Corporate Act (Chapter 617, F.S.)
    a. Demonstrate knowledge of the scope of authority of a not-for profit corporation

2. Utilize the Condominium Act (Chapter 718, F.S. and F.A.C.)
    a. Knowledge of ownership of and additional alterations to common elements
    b. Knowledge of governing document existence
    c. Knowledge of disclosure requirements
    d. Knowledge of rights, privileges, and obligations of the unit owner

3. Utilize the Florida Vacation Plan and Timesharing Act (Chapter 721, F.S.)
    a. Knowledge of record keeping and financial reporting requirements
    b. Knowledge of differences between timeshare and other forms of regulated property ownership

4. Utilize the Fair Housing Act & Americans with Disability Act
    a. Knowledge of protected categories
    b. Knowledge of familial status provisions
    c. Knowledge of physical handicap provisions
    d. Knowledge of exemption options

5. Utilize the Cooperative Act (Chapter 719, F.S. and F.A.C.)
    a. Knowledge of governing document existence
    b. Knowledge of rights, privileges, and obligations of the developer
    c. Knowledge of transition requirements

6. Utilize the Homeowners' Association Act (Chapter 720, F.S. and F.A.C.)

7. Utilize Towing Statute (Chapter 715.07, F.S.)

8. Knowledge of Association's Right of Access to Individual Units
    a. Knowledge of governing document existence
    b. Knowledge of differences among common elements, limited common elements, common areas, and association property
    c. Knowledge of cable television requirements

9. Utilize Lien Laws
    a. Knowledge of statutory and documentary assessment lien rights
    b. Knowledge of statutory and documentary construction lien rights
    c. Community Association Management, Part VIII, Chapter 468, F.S. and Chapter 61-20, F.A.C.

Community Association Management Laws

Every association is a corporation governed by a series of Florida Statutes and the Florida Administrative Code. Each association is also governed by a set of documents that are filed officially, and includes the Declaration, the Articles of Incorporation and the Bylaws of the association.

This chapter provides an overview of the various laws that affect community associations and the management of community associations. The Florida Legislative body has enacted several pieces of legislation to address the powers and authority of community associations, and provides regulations on how they are to be formed, how they operate, how voting takes place, and other management procedures.

To pass the CAM exam, you will need to be familiar with these topics and prepared with a fundamental understanding of these laws and legal concepts. We will explore the most important legal chapters of the Florida Statutes, such as Chapter 468, 718, or 720 for example, and how they relate to associations. Use the chart provided in this chapter to review and reaffirm those key laws and their primary points. These laws define the various constraints and powers which govern the authority and scope of behavior of community associations.

These are the Florida Statutes to know:

- **Chapter 607** - The Corporations Act
- **Chapter 617** - The Not For Profit Corporations Act
- **Chapter 718** - Condominiums Act
- **Chapter 719** - Cooperatives Act, aka Co-Ops
- **Chapter 720** - HOAs
- **Chapter 721** - Time-Shares
- **Chapter 723** - Mobile Homes

Along with understanding the laws that govern community associations, you must be familiar with the communities' governing documents. The governing documents are the documents which define and govern the activities and practices of the association itself, and it's members and directors. This section will explore the various Florida Statutes which govern the authority and scope of behavior of community associations.

You might have noticed how Chapters 718, 719, 720, and 721 are both in numerical and alphabetical order. This can be a handy memory-recall device. (Condos, Co-Ops, HOAs, TimeShares)

For the purposes of the CAM test, it is imperative to know the main "Chapters" presented here, and in particular you should have a comfortable familiarity with the Chapter numbers, for example - Chapter 718 is the "Condominiums" Act.

Types of Communities

There are several types of community associations, or common interest communities, such as condominiums, cooperatives, mandatory homeowners associations, and such. Every association is a corporation governed by a series of Florida Statutes and the set of documents such as the declaration, the articles of Incorporation, and the bylaws document.

The types of communities covered in the state examination and which are taught in the pre-licensure course are:

- **Condominiums**
- **Cooperatives**
- **Mandatory Homeowners Associations**
- **Time Shares**
- **Mobile Homes**

Condominiums and Co-Ops

Condominiums and cooperatives are very similar, and are usually found in the form of an apartment community, multi-family residential building, or resort type of community. The key difference between a cooperative and a condominium is the type of ownership involved for the residents.

In condominiums the owner does not technically own the unit itself, but rather owns the "airspace" within the unit. For the purposes of getting insurance and such items, the owner owns the "inside" of the unit, but not the building structure or walls. In addition to the ownership rights to the inside of the unit, condominium owners also own what is called an "undivided interest" in the common elements (or common areas, such as a Pool or Clubhouse). The ownership interests in the common elements are appurtenant to the unit, and is a part of the ownership rights. An undivided interest means that the owner of the unit owns all of the common elements that it shares in ownership with the other owners of the units within that condominium. Technically, the owner does not own a part or a fraction of the common elements. Instead, they own the entirety of the common elements and they own it in a shared fashion along with all the other members.

Cooperative home ownership (Co-Op), is a form of home ownership where the owners do not actually own the property in which they live, rather - they own shares in a corporation which is the Cooperative operating as a business entity. The entire building and often the land itself, the units, and common areas are owned by the corporation. Instead of directly owning property the individual homeowner only owns the shares in that cooperative corporation.

It is sometimes considered a less desirable form of ownership because owners do not actually own the property and it can be difficult to sell
the property because new purchasers need to be approved by the other shareholders in the corporation. In addition, there is the risk if other shareholders in the corporation are unable for some reason to contribute to the cooperative's maintenance fees, the remaining shareholders may have to cover the remainder of the needed funds.

Mandatory Homeowners Associations (HOAs)

In a Homeowner Association, or HOA, the owner typically owns the house and the parcel of property that the house is built on. The roadways and common areas are typically owned by the association as a common element or it is publicly owned by the municipality where the community sits. These common areas, such as the community pool, playground, and other facilities, are typically owned by the association, as opposed to the shared ownership that comes with condominium
common elements.

HOA's often have rules and requirements, found in the Declaration and Covenants document or other founding documents, requiring certain appearance requirements regarding landscaping and style of the home that the owner must adhere to or risk being fined. These are the main activities that people think of when HOAs are mentioned. Chapter 720 of the Florida Statutes defines the procedures and authority of homeowner associations.

Time-Shares

Time-Sharing is a form of real estate ownership where the owner has the right to possess the property for only a specified time period. The concept of time-sharing allows the owner to occupy a particular residential unit for a week or for other specific periods each year.

Some specific restrictions and rules for time-sharing to know:

- The time-share period must be for less than one year. During those other times, the other owners use the same unit for their designated time periods. Essentially, it is a shared, and scheduled, form of ownership.
- Specific standards for insurance, records keeping, exchange programs, and auditing of financial records are mandated by the Florida Statutes. For an entity to file as a time-sharing organization they must adhere to the insurance and reporting requirements.
- A timeshare purchaser, or their real estate agent, shall have access to books and records within seven days of a written request.
- Copies of the final budget shall be filed with the state within 30 days after the beginning of the fiscal year together with the reported total number of time periods of 7-day annual use which are available for sale.

Mobile Homes (Manufactured Homes)

Mobile homes, or manufactured homes, are initially considered mobile and transportable, but they are most commonly installed semi-permanently into clustered communities. For the purposes of our understanding and preparation for the test material, we are only focusing on those mobile homes which are located in mobile home "parks" or "courts".

Florida's Mobile Home Act (Chapter 723 F.S.) governs the relationship between the residents of a mobile home park community and the park owner. Chapter 723 F.S. allows for the creation of an organized association. In some circumstances, as defined specifically in Chapter 723, the association of resident mobile home owners may actually purchase the park from the owner.

If this happens, there are three options for how to organize the entity:

- Form a condominium form of ownership under Chapter 718 F.S. rules
- Form a cooperative form of ownership under Chapter 719 F.S. rules
- Form an unregulated cooperative form of ownership with a mandatory homeowners association

The formation of the association requires written consent of not less than two-thirds of all of the mobile home owners. The Mobile Home Act also gives renters a first right of refusal to purchase and provides for owners to continue to rent their unit after conversion.

Much like an HOA or Condo Association, the mobile home association shall meet once each calendar year in a public Annual Meeting and has the power to levy and collect assessments or fines.

Governing Documents

The governing documents, or founding documents, are just as important to consider as are the laws that govern community associations. The governing documents are those documents that are filed and recorded as part of the initial community creation when the entity is established. The governing documents extend the detail at which processes and community-specific matters are handled. At times the governing documents will call for specific procedures even when the statutes may not. Typically the governing documents are the first reference items which are reviewed to see how a specific procedure is handled, such as HOA architectural violations.

The governing documents are:

- The **Declaration** is the document which creates the association and specifies the rights and obligations of the members and the association. It is also referred to as the Declaration of Covenants.
- The **Articles of Incorporation** is the document filed with the Florida Department of State that creates the community association and defines its powers and responsibilities.
- **Bylaws** are the codes of rules adopted for the management of the corporation.
- **Board Rules and Regulations** are supplemental rules adopted by the association board.

Corporations Act (Chapter 607 F.S.)

This is the general corporations act and applies to all incorporated businesses in Florida, not just community associations. It provides the guidelines for how corporation entities can be formed and registered, and the requirements to continue operating year-after-year, for example - submitting Annual Reports. This is a requirement of corporations and must be filed once a year.

For corporations which are "Non-Profit", they must follow additional guidelines as defined in Chapter 617 (see next section), which applies only to Not-For-Profit corporations. For the purposes of the exam, know those two Chapter Numbers and names as you might be challenged to identify which is which.

Not-for-Profit Corporations Act

The "Not for Profit" Corporations Act is part of the Florida statutory law (Florida Statutes Chapter 617, F.S.), and outlines the rules that must be followed by not-for-profit, or non-profit corporations. It is important for a Florida CAM to know this, because the majority of these entities are registered as not-for-profit corporations.

The Condominium Act itself (which is Florida Statutes Chapter 718) requires that condominium associations must be registered as a corporation, either one that is For-Profit or Not-For-Profit. In reality, the great majority of condominium associations in Florida are registered as Not-For-Profit.

The key difference between a Non-Profit and For-Profit corporation is that in a Not-for-Profit corporation the entity's income cannot be distributed to its members, board members, committee members, or directors. For example, at the end of the year, if there are surplus funds in the budget, the directors cannot take these funds.

Articles of Incorporation

The Articles of Incorporation document, sometimes called the charter, is filed with the state when the corporate entity is created. Chapter 617 states what must be in the Articles of Incorporation: Corporate name, address, purpose of corporation, manner of electing directors, authority, range of corporate power, operating and managing corporate property, borrowing of funds, mortgaging of property, etc. Each not-for-profit corporation must have a registered agent and a registered office in the State of Florida.

Order of Priority

There may be times when there are conflicts or contradictions between two laws regarding a particular dispute. Therefore, the order of priority takes over and declares which one in the hierarchy takes precedent.

In order of priority they are:

- **Federal Constitution**
- **State Constitution**
- **Federal Statutes**
- **State Statutes**
- **Administrative Rules**
- **Local ordinances by counties and municipalities**

In addition to the statutory laws, there are also priorities among opinions and decisions by the courts. The order of priority is:

- **Supreme Court of Florida**
- **Florida District Courts of Appeals**
- **Administrative decisions and interpretations by the Division of Florida Land Sales, Condominiums and Mobile Homes**

Registered Agent

Every profit or not-for-profit corporation must have a registered agent and a registered office in the State of Florida. A registered agent, also known as a resident agent or statutory agent, is a business or individual designated to receive service of process when a business entity is a party in a legal action such as a lawsuit or summons. It is meant to be a responsible third-party who is located in the same state in which a business entity was established and who is designated to receive service of process notices, such as correspondence from the Secretary of State, or other official government notifications.

Fiduciary Obligations of Board Directors

The members of the Board of Directors, and even to some extent Committee leaders, have what is referred to as a "fiduciary" duty to perform in the best interests of those they represent.

These are the key points to remember for the examination:

- **Directors have a fiduciary obligation to perform his or her duties "In good faith"**
- **They are to perform with the care of an ordinarily prudent person in a like position would exercise under similar circumstances**
- **They are to perform in a manner he or she reasonably believes to be in the best interests of the corporation.**

Annual Condominium Unit Filing

In addition to filing the corporate annual reports, each condominium association which operates **more than two units** shall pay to the division an annual fee in the amount of $4 for each residential unit in condominiums operated by the association.

- If the fee is not paid by March 1, the association shall be assessed a penalty of 10 percent of the amount due
- The association will not have standing to maintain or defend any action in the courts of this state until the amount due plus any penalty is paid. **718.501 F.S.**

Timeshare Fees

Similar to the condominium annual filing, there is an annual fee requirement for timeshares.

- On January 1 of each year, each managing entity of a timeshare plan located in Florida shall collect as a common expense and pay to the division an annual fee of **$2 for each 7 days** of annual use availability that exist within the timeshare plan at that time, subject to any limitations on the amount of such annual fee.
- If any portion of the annual fee is not paid by March 1, the association may be assessed a penalty.

Governing Documents

The governing documents consist of the Declaration, the Bylaws document, the Articles of Incorporation, and the Board's Rules and Regulations.

The Declaration of Covenants

The declaration is usually the largest of the governing documents and contains most of the guidelines and founding information for the setup of the association The Declaration contains a legal description of the property that is subject to the authority of the declaration and the association. It provides the foundation for the whole structure of the association.

The Declaration contains:

- Definitions of the terms used in the declaration
- Descriptions of the legal boundaries of the units in a condominium association
- Description of procedures for voting, meetings, and adopting amendments
- Management guidelines for the Board
- Description of the process and formulas used to determine assessments
- Declares what the occupancy and use restrictions are

Bylaws and the Board's Rules

As the declaration serves to provide the foundational guidelines for the association, the next level of detail is provided in the Bylaws document, and then finally the Board's Rules and Regulations. The bylaws and rules and regulations often contain the association's quorum and voting requirements, meeting requirements, powers and duties of the board, and the manner for budgeting and collecting assessments.

At this level the guidelines are provided for what types of meetings must be held, the makeup of the board in relation to the number of directors and officers that serve, descriptions of the roles of the officers, voting requirements, and other requirements concerning the governance of the association.

Table - Florida Statutes - The Florida Statutes which will be covered in the examination are listed below. Please become familiar with these chapters, and know the corresponding number for each.

Chapter 607 - General Corporations Act	
	Chapter 607 of the Florida Statutes defines the scope and authority of corporations registered in Florida.
Chapter 617 - Corporations Not-for-Profit	
	Chapter 617 of the Florida Statutes defines the scope and authority of "Not-For-Profit" corporations registered in Florida.
Chapter 718 - Condominiums Act	
	The Condominiums Act is Chapter 718 of the Florida Statutes. "Condominium" means individual ownership of a unit coupled with joint ownership of an undivided share of the common elements. Condominium ownership means: • Exclusive (individual) ownership of a unit • Joint ownership of the common elements • Membership in the association **PART I -** **General Provisions** Provisions for creation of a condominium and the day-to-day operations. This is the most used part. **PART II -** **Rights and Obligations of Developers** Rights and obligations of the developer including maximum statutory warranties of three years from completion of building or one year from transition. **PART III -** **Rights and Obligations of Associations** Covers transition, rights of the association to cancel agreements, establishes the content of maintenance and management agreements and provides for the prevailing party to get court costs and attorney fees. **PART IV -** **Special Types of Condominiums** Describes special types of condominiums: leasehold estate, conversions and adding of

phases.

PART V –
Regulation and Disclosure Prior to Sale of Residential Condominiums Provides for regulation by the Division of Florida Condominiums, Timeshares and Mobile Homes. Mandates disclosure requirements, prospectus, and provides for a filing fee of $20 per unit for developer for each unit offered to sell and $4 per unit, annually, for association after turnover.

PART VI –
Conversions to Condominiums Conversions from rental to condominium and protection for renters. Provides tenants the option to extend current rental agreements, and right of refusal to purchase their unit. Developer to establish reserve accounts for capital expenditures and deferred maintenance or give warranties or post a surety bond.

Chapter 719 - Cooperatives Act

Chapter 719 of the Florida Statutes is the Cooperatives Act, known also as the "Co-Op" Act.

"Cooperative" means the cooperative entity owns the units and the common elements. Cooperative ownership means:

- Legal title of the unit is vested in the cooperative
- Ownership of the common elements is with the cooperative
- Membership in the association includes the right to use of individual unit

PART I -
General Provisions
Creates the cooperative and provides guidelines for the rights and responsibilities of the association and its members. Halts statute of limitations until members gain control.

PART II –
Rights and Obligations of Developers Developers rights and responsibilities (escrowing for taxes and special assessments, disclosure for purchase agreements) and warranties (usually three years and no longer than five).

PART III -
Rights and Obligations of Associations Covers transition and rights and obligations of the association, including the right to cancel agreements and provides for prevailing party to get court costs and attorney fees.

PART IV -
Special Types of Cooperatives Describes special types of cooperatives, leaseholds, conversions and adding of phases to an existing cooperative.

PART V -
Regulation and Disclosure Prior to Sale of Residential Cooperatives Provides for regulation by the department of Florida Land Sales, Condominiums and Mobile Homes. Mandates disclosure requirements and annual fees.

PART VI -
Conversions to Cooperatives Conversions from rental to cooperative and protection for renters. Developer to furnish warranties as if new and to establish reserves. In addition, developer to furnish statements as to soundness, etc. of existing structure to purchasers.

Chapter 720 - Mandatory Homeowners' Association Act (HOA Act)

Chapter 720 of the Florida Statutes is the HOA Act.

Part I –
General Provisions Almost all of the information normally used to manage a HOA is located in this part.

Part II –
Disclosure Prior to the Sale of Residential Parcels Covers developer's disclosure requirements.

Part III –
Covenant Revitalization Provides guidance for reviving an association.

Chapter 721 - Time Sharing Act	
	Chapter 721 of the Florida Statutes is the Time Sharing Act This legislation covers a narrow scope of special condominiums, cooperatives, and other types of residential properties. Time-sharing is not permitted in condos or co-ops unless special provisions were provided in the declaration-of-condominium or the cooperative documents. The concept of time-sharing allows the owner to occupy a particular residential unit for a week or for other specific periods each year. The time-share period must be for less than one year. Other owners use the same unit for other time periods. Specific standards for insurance, records keeping, exchange programs, and auditing of financial records are mandated. A purchaser, or their agent, shall have access to books and records within seven days of a written request. Copies of the final budget shall be filed with the division within 30 days after-beginning of the fiscal year together with the number of periods of 7-day annual use available.
Chapter 723 **Mobile Homes**	**Mobile Home Act** Governs the arrangements of residential living between the residents of a mobile home park and the park owner. The mobile home act allows for the creation of an association and under some circumstances, it may actually purchase the park from the owner. When they do, they have three choices: • Form a condominium form of ownership under 718 • Form a cooperative form of ownership under 719 • Form an unregulated cooperative form of ownership with a mandatory homeowners association The formation of the association requires written consent of not less than two-thirds of all of the mobile home owners. The Act also gives renters a first right of refusal to purchase and provides for owners to continue to rent their unit after conversion. The association shall meet once each calendar year and that meeting shall be the annual meeting. The association has the power to make, levy and collect assessments.

Condominium Act (Chapter 718, F.S. and F.A.C.)

The Condominiums Act is Chapter 718 of the Florida Statutes, and it contains 6 parts which define the power and authority of condominiums. "Condominium" means individual ownership of a unit coupled with joint ownership of an undivided share of the common elements. Condominium ownership means:

- Exclusive (individual) ownership of a unit
- Joint ownership of the common elements
- Membership in the association

PART I – General Provisions Provisions for creation of a condominium and the day-to-day operations. This is the most used part.

PART II – Rights and Obligations of Developers Rights and obligations of the developer including maximum statutory warranties of three years from completion of building or one year from transition.

PART III – Rights and Obligations of Associations Covers transition, rights of the association to cancel agreements, establishes the content of maintenance and management agreements and provides for the prevailing party to get court costs and attorney fees.

PART IV – Special Types of Condominiums Describes special types of condominiums: leasehold estate, conversions and adding of phases.

PART V – Regulation and Disclosure Prior to Sale of Residential Condominiums Provides for regulation by the Division of Florida Condominiums, Timeshares and Mobile Homes. Mandates disclosure requirements, prospectus, and provides for a filing fee of $20 per unit for developer for each unit offered to sell and $4 per unit, annually, for association after turnover.

PART VI – Conversions to Condominiums Conversions from rental to condominium and protection for renters. Provides tenants the option to extend current rental agreements, and right of refusal to purchase their unit. Developer to establish reserve accounts for capital expenditures and deferred maintenance or give warranties or post a surety bond.

Ownership of and additional alterations to common elements

As a condominium unit owner, there are also rights and appurtenances that come with the unit. A condominium parcel is a unit, together with the undivided s "appurtenant" to the unit. It is created by the declaration and is a separate parcel of real property that can be bought and sold. Appurtenances are things that belong to and go with something else, the appurtenance being less significant than what it belongs to, such as a Parking space.

Per the Condominium Act, appurtenances to a condominium unit is defined as:

- An undivided share in the common elements and common surplus (The common surplus are the excess funds of the association after payment of all its expenses).
- The exclusive right to use such portion of the common elements as may be provided by the declaration.
- An exclusive easement for the use of the airspace occupied by the unit.
- Membership in the association designated in the declaration, with the full voting rights appertaining thereto.
- Other appurtenances as may be provided in the declaration per Chapter 718 of the Florida Statutes.

The rights and appurtenances of a condominium owner cannot be separated from the unit, and cannot be sold separately. For example, the condo unit owner cannot sell their parking space.

Governing document existence

Condominiums in Florida are established pursuant to Chapter 718, the Condominium Act. The condominium is created when the Declarations are recorded in the county where it is located. Definitions concerns unit size or changes are governed by the declarations.

Amendments are possible though. These are the guidelines to know:

- Communities must follow their own rules and any relevant laws before taking certain actions such as amending the declaration.
- A certain number of members, or board members, must be present for a vote to be valid, and different types of decisions may require different numbers of votes.

If the terms to an amendment is voted and agreed upon, then it must be recorded in the county in order to make it official.

Disclosure requirements

Florida laws protect consumers who are purchasing condominium units with a set of required disclosure documents which must be provided to prospective buyers. Associations that can levy assessments and fines should be given background information about the community association before they make a purchase.

The level of disclosure required by a developer of a new residential condominium differs from that of a non-developer. Disclosure by a seller in an HOA is also different from the condominium requirements. Developer-level disclosure in the sale of new residential condominiums is the largest and most comprehensive.

Developer's disclosure requirements:

- For the sale of a residential unit or a lease thereof for an unexpired term of more than 5 years, Chapter 718 requires the contract contain notification to the buyer that the agreement is voidable within 15 days after the execution of the contract.
- The developer must also disclose if the unit has been occupied by someone other than the buyer.
- If the contract is for the sale or transfer of a unit subject to a lease.
- If the contract is for the lease of a unit for a term of 5 years or more.
- If the contract is for the sale or lease of a unit that is subject to a lien for rent payable under a lease of a recreational facility or other commonly used facility.
- Must state the name and address of the escrow agent.
- Disclose whether timeshare estates have been or may be created.

Each prospective purchaser who has entered into a contract for the purchase of a condominium unit is entitled, at the seller's expense, to the following items.

Unit Seller's disclosure requirements:

- A current copy of the declaration of condominium
- Articles of incorporation of the association
- Bylaws and rules of the association
- financial information,
- FAQs Document
- Governance form

Rights, privileges, and obligations of the unit owner

There are rights, privileges, and obligations of the unit owner and a specific process for the handling of complaints.

- When a unit owner files a written inquiry by certified mail with the board of administration, the board shall respond in writing to the unit owner within 30 days of receipt of the inquiry.
- The board's response shall either give a substantive response to the inquirer, notify the inquirer that a legal opinion has been requested, or notify the inquirer that advice has been requested from the division. **718.112 F.S.**

Developer's Warranties:

- The developer shall be deemed to have granted to the purchaser of each unit an implied warranty of fitness and merchantability for the purposes or uses intended as to each unit, a warranty for 3 years commencing with the completion of the building containing the unit. **718.203 F.S.**
- After transferring ownership of a condominium association to the members, developer warranties for first time purchasers continue to run for 1 year. **718.203 F.S.**

The Florida Vacation Plan and Timesharing Act (Chapter 721, F.S.)

Chapter 721 of the Florida Statutes is the "Time-Sharing" Act. This legislation covers a narrow scope of special condominiums, cooperatives, and other types of residential properties. Time-sharing is not permitted in condos or co-ops unless special provisions were provided in the declaration-of-condominium or the cooperative documents. The concept of time-sharing allows the owner to occupy a particular residential unit for a week or for other specific periods each year. The time-share period must be for less than one year. Other owners use the same unit for other time periods.

Specific standards for insurance, records keeping, exchange programs, and auditing of financial records are mandated. A purchaser, or their agent, shall have access to books and records within seven days of a written request. Copies of the final budget shall be filed with the division within 30 days after-beginning of the fiscal year together with the number of periods of 7-day annual use available.

Record keeping and financial reporting requirements

The Florida Vacation Plan and Timesharing Act give statutory recognition and authority to real property timeshare plans and personal property timeshare plans. They establish the procedures for the creation, sale, exchange, promotion, and operation of timeshare plans. They provide full and fair disclosure to current purchasers and prospective buyers of timeshare plans.

It is a requirement that every timeshare plan offered for sale or created and existing in this state to be subjected to the provisions of this chapter.

A "Timeshare plan" means any arrangement, plan, scheme, or similar device, other than an exchange program, whether by membership, agreement, tenancy in common, sale, lease, deed, rental agreement, license, or right-to-use agreement or by any other means, whereby a purchaser, for consideration, receives ownership rights in or a right to use accommodations, and facilities, if any, for a period of time less than a full year during any given year, but not necessarily for consecutive years.

Timeshare Plan Seller's Requirements:

- A copy of each contract for the sale of a timeshare interest
- If a timeshare estate is being sold, the seller is required to retain a copy of the contract only until a deed of conveyance, agreement for deed, or lease is recorded in the office of the clerk of the circuit court in the county wherein the plan is located
- If a personal property timeshare plan is being sold, the seller is required to retain a copy of the contract only until a certificate of transfer is available
- A list of all salespersons of the seller and their last known addresses. The names and addresses of such salespersons whose employments terminate shall be retained for 3 years after termination of employment
- If the seller has a contract with any entity not owned or controlled by the seller for the sale of the timeshare plan, that entity shall be responsible for maintaining a record of current employees involved in the sale of the timeshare plan and a record of any former employees involved in the sale of such plan within the previous 3 years

The management company or association has a duty to keep records available and has to fulfill specific financial reporting guidelines.

The duties of the manager include:

- Each year the management firm shall provide to all purchasers an itemized annual budget which shall include all estimated revenues and expenses
- The budget shall be the final budget adopted by the managing entity for the current fiscal year
- A copy of the final budget shall be filed with the division for review within 30 days after the beginning of each fiscal year

The Fair Housing Act (FHA) and the Americans-with-Disability Act (ADA)

The Federal Fair Housing Act makes it unlawful to discriminate because of race, color, national origin, sex, handicap, religion, or familial status. Familial Status is defined as families with children under the age of 18.

There are some provisions for retirement communities, also referred to as "55+" communities, which are the exception:

- Must be registered with the Florida Commission on Human Resources, and
- Must be intended for and solely occupied by persons 62 years or older, or,
- When occupancy is restricted to residents 55 years of age or older, Must be intended and operated for occupancy by at least one person 55 years or over per unit and at least 80 percent of the parcels are occupied by at least one person 55 years of age or over.

In addition to the Federal Fair Housing Act, Florida has its own fair housing act. However, in the state version, Florida does not provide for the familial status protection, only the others. For the purpose of the Fair Housing Act: Handicap is defined as a physical or mental impairment which substantially limits one or more of a person's major life activities.

Protected categories

From a legal standpoint these are the specific classes, or categories of identifiers upon which the legislation is based and is aimed to protect.
The protected classes under the FHA are:

- race
- color
- religion
- sex
- handicap
- familial status
- national origin

Familial Status

Familial status is one of the protected classes under the Fair Housing Act. Familial status means one or more individuals (who have not attained the age of 18 years) and living with:

- A parent or another person having legal custody of such individual or individuals
- The designee of such parent or other person having such custody with their written permission

Physical handicap provisions

There are legal protections for persons with disabilities. A person with a disability is defined as any person who has a physical or mental impairment that substantially limits one or more major life activities, has a record of such impairment, or is regarded as having such an impairment.

It is unlawful to discriminate in the sale or rental, or to otherwise make unavailable or deny, a dwelling to any buyer or renter because of a handicap of that buyer or renter, of a person residing in or intending to reside in that dwelling after it is sold, rented, or made available, or of any person associated with that buyer or renter.

Exemption options

In some cases, full compliance with the FHA is not required, as the laws were designed to target commercial and corporate entities and not so much the small, private landlord.

Exemptions where FHA compliance is not required:

- Owner occupied buildings with no more than four units.
- A building may be exempt from the provisions of the Fair Housing Act related to familial status if at least 80 percent of the occupied units are occupied by at least one person who is 55 years of age or older.
- Single family housing sold or rented without the use of a broker if the private individual owner does not own more than three such single family homes at one time.
- Housing operated by organizations and private clubs that limit occupancy to members
- A House sold or rented by an owner who does not own more than three single-family houses, and does not reside in such house.

The Cooperative Act (Chapter 719, F.S. and F.A.C.)

A "Cooperative" means that form of ownership of real property wherein legal title is vested in a corporation or other entity and the beneficial use is evidenced by an ownership interest in the association and a lease or other muniment of title or possession granted by the association as the owner of all the cooperative property.

Chapter 719 of the Florida Statutes is the Cooperatives Act, known also as the "Co-Op" Act. Cooperative refers to the cooperative entity owns the units and the common elements.

Key points to remember for Cooperative ownership:

- Legal title of the unit is vested in the cooperative
- Ownership of the common elements is with the cooperative
- Membership in the association includes the right to use of individual unit

The Co-Op Act is large and contains several parts:

PART I - General Provisions
Creates the cooperative and provides guidelines for the rights and responsibilities of the association and its members. Halts statute of limitations until members gain control.

PART II - Rights and Obligations of Developers
Developers rights and responsibilities (escrowing for taxes and special assessments, disclosure for purchase agreements) and warranties (usually three years and no longer than five).

PART III - Rights and Obligations of Associations
Covers transition and rights and obligations of the association, including the right to cancel agreements and provides for prevailing party to get court costs and attorney fees.

PART IV - Special Types of Cooperatives
Describes special types of cooperatives, leaseholds, conversions and adding of phases to an existing cooperative.

PART V - Regulation and Disclosure Prior to Sale of Residential Cooperatives
Provides for regulation by the department of Florida Land Sales, Condominiums and Mobile Homes. Mandates disclosure requirements and annual fees.

PART VI - Conversions to Cooperatives
Conversions from rental to cooperative and protection for renters. Developer to furnish warranties as if new and to establish reserves. In addition, developer to furnish statements as to soundness, etc. of existing structure to purchasers.

Governing document existence

The cooperative is started when the corporation documents are recorded and filed with the Department of State. The cooperative documents must be recorded in the county in which the cooperative is located before property may be conveyed or transferred to the cooperative.

Obligations of the developer, per Chapter 719 Florida Statutes:

- If a developer contracts to sell a cooperative parcel and the construction, furnishing, and landscaping of the property submitted or proposed to be submitted to cooperative ownership has not been substantially completed in accordance with the plans and specifications and representations made by the developer in the disclosures required by this chapter, the developer shall pay into an escrow account all payments up to 10 percent of the sale price received by the developer from the buyer towards the sale price.
- The escrow agent shall give to the purchaser a receipt for the deposit, upon request. In lieu of the foregoing, the division director shall have the discretion to accept other assurances, including, but not limited to, a surety bond or an irrevocable letter of credit in an amount equal to the escrow requirements of this section.

Transition requirements

Chapter 719 of the Florida Statutes dictates the process by which the developer transitions the association to the members. The process of "transition" refers to the transfer from developer-control of a community association to the establishment of a member-controlled association. At the start of any common interest community, before any lots or condos are sold, the developer owns all the units. A developer is a person who buys and develops houses, buildings, and land in order to sell them and make a profit from them.

When the community is initially founded, the developer is responsible for putting all of the legal structures in place for the type of community that is being built. Therefore, the developer is the one who will put into place the governing documents and have those documents recorded in the county where the property is located.

As the community is developed, units or lots will be sold to new owners. During this period, the developer retains control (voting majority) over the association that has been put into place, but as the properties begin to move from being primarily developer-owned to resident-owned, the voting power and management authority eventually transitions to the residents of the community.

Transition is said to occur when **15% or more** of the units to be operated by the association are owned by non-developer owners. Once this happens, the non-developer **unit owners** are entitled to elect not less than one-third of the members of the board.

- **3 years** after 50 percent of the units that will be operated ultimately by the association have been conveyed to purchasers
- **3 months** after 90 percent of the units that will be operated ultimately by the association have been conveyed to purchasers
- When all the units that will be operated ultimately by the association have been completed
- When some of the units have been conveyed to purchasers and none of the others are being constructed or offered for sale by the developer in the ordinary course of business, or **7 years** after creation of the cooperative association, whichever occurs first.

The Homeowners' Association Act (Chapter 720, F.S. and F.A.C.)

Chapter 720 of the Florida Statutes defines "Homeowners' Association" or "association" to mean a Florida corporation responsible for the operation of a community or a mobile home subdivision in which the voting membership is made up of parcel owners or their agents, or a combination thereof, and in which membership is a mandatory condition of parcel ownership, and which is authorized to impose assessments that, if unpaid, may become a lien on the parcel.

The incorporation rules for HOAs are:

- They must be operated by an association that is a Florida corporation, cannot be a Delaware corporation or other state
- Incorporated and the initial governing documents must be recorded in the official records of the county in which the community is located
- An association may operate more than one community
- The officers and directors of an association have a fiduciary relationship to the members who are served by the association

The powers and duties of an association include those set forth both in Chapter 720 and in the governing documents. After control of the association is obtained by members other than the developer, the association may institute, maintain, settle, or appeal actions or hearings in its name as an independent entity.

Record Keeping

The association manager has a duty to retain records for archival purposes. The following items are recommended to be kept, for a period of at least 7 Years:

- A copy of the bylaws of the association and of each amendment to the bylaws
- A copy of the articles of incorporation of the association and any amendments
- A copy of the declaration of covenants and a copy of any amendments
- A copy of the current rules of the homeowners' association
- The minutes of all meetings of the board of directors and of the members must be retained for at least 7 years
- A current roster of all member persons and their property/parcel identification

- All of the association's insurance policies, these must be retained for at least 7 years.
- A current copy of all contracts or lawsuits to which the association is a party
- The financial and accounting records of the association, kept according to good accounting practices. All financial and accounting records must be maintained for a period of at least 7 years

Prohibited Clauses in Association Documents per Chapter 720

It is declared that the public policy of this state prohibits the inclusion or enforcement of certain types of clauses in homeowners' association documents, including declaration of covenants, articles of incorporation, bylaws, or any other document of the association which binds members of the association, which either have the effect of or provide that:

- A developer has the unilateral ability and right to make changes to the homeowners' association documents after the transition of homeowners' association control in a community from the developer to the non-developer members, as set forth in s. 720.307, has occurred.

- A homeowners' association is prohibited or restricted from filing a lawsuit against the developer, or the homeowners' association is otherwise effectively prohibited or restricted from bringing a lawsuit against the developer.

- After the transition of homeowners' association control in a community from the developer to the non-developer members, as set forth in s. 720.307, has occurred, a developer is entitled to cast votes in an amount that exceeds one vote per residential lot. **Chapter 720 F.S.**

Utilize Towing Statute (Chapter 715.07, F.S.)

Chapter 715 of the Florida Statutes sets forth the guidelines for towing of vehicles:

"The owner or lessee of real property, or any person authorized by the owner or lessee, which person may be the designated representative of the condominium association if the real property is a condominium, may cause any vehicle or vessel parked on such property without her or his permission to be removed by a person regularly engaged in the business of towing vehicles or vessels, without liability for the costs of removal, transportation, or storage or damages caused by such removal, transportation, or storage, under any of the following circumstances:

- The towing or removal of any vehicle or vessel from private property without the consent of the registered owner or other legally authorized person in control of that vehicle or vessel is subject to strict compliance with the following conditions and restrictions.
- Any towed or removed vehicle or vessel must be stored at a site within a 10-mile radius of the point of removal in any county of 500,000 population or more, and within a 15-mile radius of the point of removal in any county of less than 500,000 population.
- That site must be open for the purpose of redemption of vehicles on any day that the person or firm towing such vehicle or vessel is open for towing purposes, from 8:00 a.m. to 6:00 p.m., and, when closed, shall have prominently posted a sign indicating a telephone number where the operator of the site can be reached at all times.
- Upon receipt of a telephoned request to open the site to redeem a vehicle or vessel, the operator shall return to the site within 1 hour or she or he will be in violation of this section." **Chapter 715.07 F.S.**

The Association's Right of Access to Individual Units

In both condominiums and cooperatives, the association has the right to access each unit during reasonable hours when necessary for maintenance, repair, or replacement. The purpose of this rule is to ensure that uncooperative owners cannot prevent necessary repairs that could damage association property or the property and units of other owners. Without this rule, one owner's refusal to make necessary repairs could cause disastrous effects to association and its members.

Defining common areas

Association managers must be familiar with the differences among common elements, limited common elements, common areas, and association property. The common elements are defined as the portions of the condominium or cooperative property not included in the units. **Limited common elements** are the elements or areas which are reserved for the use of a certain unit or units to the exclusion of all other units, as specified in the declaration or community documents.

Cable television requirements for Co-Ops and Condos

Cooperatives have specific provisions regarding cable television. When they order services from a cable TV provider, they can enter into a bulk agreement. A bulk contract entered into by the association is deemed a common expense.

- The contract must be for at least two years
- Any contract made by the board after April 2, 1992 may be canceled by a majority of the voting interests present at the next regular or special meeting
- Hearing impaired or legally blind unit owners who do not occupy the unit with a nonhearing impaired or sight person may discontinue service and are exempted from having to pay the common expenses associated with the service

"Condominiums cannot deny owners or tenants the right to access franchised or licensed cable television service, nor may they require payment to obtain such service other than those charges normally paid for like services by residents of, or providers of such services, to single-family homes within the same franchised or licensed area, except for installation charges as such charges may be agreed to between such resident and the provider of such services." **Chapter 718 F.S.**

Lien Laws

The ability to impose liens is a powerful tool that associations have to ensure that delinquent homeowners, who have not paid their assessments, are contributing fairly with their share of the costs. A lien is a right to keep possession of property belonging to another person until a debt owed by that person is discharged. The law allows associations to take possession of the units or properties of homeowners within the association if they failed to pay their assessments. This is essentially similar to the lien rights that a bank has on a mortgaged property. If the monthly mortgage payments are not made, the bank can start the process to take the home back.

Construction Liens

A construction lien, also known as a mechanic's lien, is a mechanism that certain types of vendors use to collect payment for work and materials, from the people that hire them to perform construction services but have not paid for them.

Community Associations and Managers (Chapter 468 F.S.)

The examination will contain several questions on matters dealing with Chapter 468 of the Florida Statutes, so ensure that you are familiar with them and their purpose. Here we will explore the regulations found in **Community Association Management, Part VIII, Chapter 468, F.S. and Chapter 61- 20, F.A.C.** These are the specific definitions as to what community associations and community association managers are.

Community Associations and Chapter 468

A community association is defined as a "residential homeowners' association in which membership is a condition of ownership of a unit in a planned unit development, or of a lot for a home or a mobile home, or of a townhouse, villa, condominium, cooperative, or other residential unit which is part of a residential development scheme and which is authorized to impose a fee which may become a lien on the parcel."

"Community association management" means any of the following practices requiring substantial specialized knowledge, judgment, and managerial skill when done for payment, and when the association served contains more than 10 units or has an annual budget in excess of $100,000:

- Controlling or disbursing funds of a community association,
- Preparing budgets or other financial documents for a community association
- Assisting in the noticing processing or conducting of community association meetings
- Determining the number of days required for statutory notices
- Determining amounts due to the association
- Collecting amounts due to the association
- Calculating the votes required for a quorum or to approve a proposition or amendment
- Completing forms related to the management of a community association that have been created by statute or by a state agency
- Drafting meeting notices and agendas
- Calculating and preparing certificates of assessment and estoppel certificates
- Responding to requests for certificates of assessment and estoppel certificates

- Negotiating monetary or performance terms of a contract subject to approval by an association
- Drafting pre-arbitration demands

- Coordinating or performing maintenance for real or personal property and other related routine services involved in the operation of a community association,
- Complying with the association's governing documents and the requirements of law as necessary to perform such practices.

"Community association management firm" means a corporation, limited liability company, partnership, trust, association, sole proprietorship, or other similar organization engaging in the business of community association management for the purpose of providing any of the services listed above from Chapter 468 F.S.

Helpful Tip

A person who performs clerical or ministerial functions, such as an administrative assistant, under the direct supervision and control of a licensed manager; or who is charged only with performing the maintenance of a community association and who does not assist in any of the management services described in this subsection, is not required to be licensed under this part.

The Licensure Rules in Chapter 468

Licensure of community association managers and community association management firms:

- A person shall not manage or hold herself or himself out to the public as being able to manage a community association in this state unless she or he is licensed by the department in accordance with the provisions of this part. However, nothing in this part prohibits any person licensed in this state under any other law or court rule from engaging in the profession for which she or he is Licensed.

- As of January 1, 2009, a community association management firm or other similar organization responsible for the management of more than 10 units or a budget of $100,000 or greater shall not engage or hold itself out to the public as being able to engage in the business of community association management in this state unless it is licensed by the department as a community association management firm in accordance with the provisions of this part.

- A community association management firm or other similar organization desiring to be licensed as a community association management firm shall apply to the department on a form approved by the department, together with the application and licensure fees required by s.468.435(1)(a) and (c).

- Each community association management firm applying for licensure under this subsection must be actively registered and authorized to do business in this state.

- Each applicant shall designate on its application a licensed community association manager who shall be required to respond to all inquiries from and investigations by the department or division.

- Each licensed community association management firm shall notify the department within 30 days after any change of information contained in the application upon which licensure is based.

- Community association management firm licenses shall expire on September 30 of odd-numbered years and shall be renewed every 2 years. An application for renewal shall be accompanied by the renewal fee as required by s. 468.435(1)(d).

- The department shall license each applicant whom the department certifies as meeting the requirements of this subsection.

- If the license of at least one individual active community association manager member is not in force, the license of the community association management firm or other similar organization is canceled automatically during that time.

- Any community association management firm or other similar organization agrees by being licensed that it will employ only licensed persons in the direct provision of community association management services as described in s. 468.431(3).

Continuing Education Requirements for CAMs

In order to maintain an active CAM license, the licensee must confirm the following before the renewal deadline:

- Completion of 20 hours during the biennium (2 years) prior to the license renewal date. The courses required are in the following areas:
    - 4 hours of legal update seminars
    - 4 hours on insurance and financial management topics relating to community association management
    - 4 hours on the operation of the association's physical property
    - 4 hours on human resources topics relating to community association management - topics may include, but are not limited to, disaster preparedness, employee relations, and communications skills for effectively dealing with residents and vendors

- 4 hours of additional instruction in any area described in Rule 61-20.508(3)(b),(c) or (d) Florida Administrative Code or any course or courses directly related to the management or administration of community associations.

Part II - Procedures (25%)

This section covers 25% of the test material, so be sure to familiarize yourself well with this material. "Procedures" refers to the practice of conducting meetings, and providing Notices for those meetings.

EXAM TOPICS FOR PART II - NOTICING, AND CONDUCTING MEETINGS

1. Notice procedures for the Association and Board Meetings
   a. Knowledge of types of meetings
   b. Knowledge of requirements of conducting a meeting (Association membership and special meetings, and meetings of the Board)
   c. Knowledge of proof of notice of meeting
   d. Knowledge of agenda requirements
   e. Knowledge of proxy requirements
   f. Knowledge of voting and abstaining from voting
   g. Knowledge of minutes and records requirements
   h. Knowledge of election process, recall, and filling vacancies upon resignation
   i. Knowledge of quorum requirements
   j. Knowledge of scope of authority of association officers and directors
   k. Knowledge of notice content, posting, delivery requirements for board and association members

2. Facilitate Committee Operations
   a. Knowledge of creation of committees
   b. Knowledge of scope of authority
   c. Knowledge of notice, agenda, and procedures
   d. Knowledge of development and understanding of committee reports
   e. Knowledge of search committee functions

3. Knowledge of Voting Procedures
   a. Knowledge of governing document existence
   b. Knowledge of balloting
   c. Knowledge of developer rights and privileges
   d. Knowledge of transition members' meeting
   e. Knowledge of eligibility requirements
   f. Knowledge of voting certificates

Notice procedures for the Association and Board Meetings

Community associations host and facilitate a number of meetings and votes throughout the year. The duties of each officer of the Board of Directors are set forth in the by-laws of the association. The Board of Directors sets forth the policies of the association and management carries out that policy.

The Board of Directors has a "fiduciary" responsibility to the community to administer the association in the best possible way and to protect the assets of the community. It's important for the community association manager to adhere to all the regulations and guidelines regarding how to conduct meetings, make prior announcements with plenty of time, and maintain proper quorums for voting sessions.

Types of meetings

The most common meetings are the Annual Owners Meeting, Special Owners Meeting, Monthly Board Business Meeting, and Committee Meetings. All meetings must be property announced (ie, "Noticed") and business dealings must be transparent so as to minimize conflicts and unethical practices.

Types of meetings:

- **Annual Owners Meeting** (General meeting of the entire assembly)
- **Special Owners Meeting**
- **Monthly Board Business Meeting**
- **Committee Meetings**

Requirements of conducting a meeting

(Association membership and special meetings, and meetings of the Board)

As a member of the association, the owner has a right to hear the issues, participate in the decisions, elect representatives to lead, and approve budgets and assessments. To facilitate this, Florida Statutes define how meeting procedures should be announced and documented.

Requirements of conducting a meeting (Association membership and special meetings, and meetings of the Board)

- General membership meetings, including Special Owner's Meetings, cannot be held without proper notice to all of the owners.
- A member can waive notice, but the waiver must be in writing and the authority to waive must be in the documents.
- The notice shall be mailed, hand delivered, or electronically transmitted at least 14 days prior to the meeting.
- Posting the notice on property 14 days prior to the meeting is required for condominiums.
- HOAs may adopt a procedure to conspicuously post or broadcast the notice on closed-circuit television in lieu of other notices.

Emergency Powers

In times of emergency, the association may employ special powers for the safety of the community. For example, to turn off the gas to a condo unit in the event of a hurricane.

Upon declaration of a state of emergency by the Governor of Florida in the locale where the association is located, the Board may, but is not required to, exercise certain powers in response to damage caused by the emergency.

- Conduct Board and Membership meeting with notice given as is practicable
- Cancel and reschedule any association meeting
- Designate assistant officer who are not directors
- Relocate the association's principal office
- Enter into agreements with counties/municipalities for debris removal
- Implement a disaster plan which may include shutting down elevators, electricity, water, sewer or security systems
- Require evacuation of association property and, upon the advice of professionals, determine any portion of the property is unavailable for entry
- Contract, on behalf of unit owners, for items or services for which the owners are otherwise individually responsible for but which are necessary to prevent further damage to the association property
- Levy special assessments without a vote of the owners
- Without owners' approval, borrow money and pledge association assets as collateral to fund emergency repairs and carry out the duties of the association when the operating funds are insufficient
- The above powers are limited to that time reasonably necessary to protect the health, safety, and welfare of the association and the parcel owners and their family members, tenants, guests, agents, or invitees, and to mitigate further damage and make emergency repairs.

Proof-of-Notice of meetings

One of the key obligations of proper association administration is the fair and timely notices given prior to meetings taking place, so that everyone gets a chance to participate. Especially if budget approvals, special assessments, or board members are being voted on. Proof-of-Notice of meetings is a required document process and archiving activity that managers must do. They must follow the proper deadlines in providing upcoming notice of a meeting, and should keep long-term records to demonstrate that proper notice has always been provided.

Helpful Tip

Later in this chapter there is a table of Meeting Requirements and proof-of-notice requirements for various types of association meetings. Get to know the chart well and memorize the contents for the examination as best you can!

For the examination, remember these key points regarding owners' meetings, per the Florida Statutes:

- General membership meetings cannot be held without proper notice to all of the owners. The notice of the meeting must contain the date, location, time, and purpose of the meeting.
- A member can waive notice, but the waiver must be in writing and the authority to waive must be in the governing documents
- The notice can be mailed, hand delivered, or electronically-transmitted; but must be sent at least 14 days prior to the meeting
- Posting the notice on property 14 days prior to the meeting is a requirement for condominiums
- HOAs may adopt a procedure to conspicuously post or broadcast the notice on closed-circuit television in lieu of other notices. If broadcast notice is used in lieu of physically posting the notice, the notice and agenda must be broadcast at least four times every broadcast hour of each day that a posted notice is required
- If amendments are to be voted on at the meeting, then copies of the amendments proposed must also accompany the notice of the meeting

Meeting agenda requirements

As general attendance is recommended for members for most meetings, it is particularly important to get a proper voice at certain meetings, such as the annual budget meeting. Specific guidelines have been put in place to address the disclosure of upcoming meeting agendas to the members.

For the purposes of the examination, remember these meeting agenda requirements:

- The standard notice for a meeting must contain the time, date, place and the purpose of the meeting. This is used for regular board of directors meetings, an annual owners' meeting to elect directors, etc.
- However, if a budget or special assessment is on the table, in that case a copy of the budget must also accompany the notice, and a special meeting to approve a special assessment is announced. In addition, note that **14** days notice is required.
- If the special assessment is to be approved, then the notice of the assessment must include the amount, date of payment and date of delinquency.
- Notices for membership meetings for a homeowners' association will be provided as called for in the bylaws. If not specified in the bylaws, notice must be given not less than 14 days prior to the meeting.
- Chapter 617 dictates that notice be sent out at least ten days before the meeting and no longer than sixty days before the meeting. Chapters 718, 719, and 723 require at least 14 days notice.
- The most stringent requirement prevails, so in a condominium, cooperative, or mobile home park, notice must be given at least 14 days and no longer than 60 days prior to the members meeting.

Proxy requirements

Proxy voting is the process by which a substitute party is designated to provide a vote on behalf of an association member. In the case of proxy voting, there are different requirements, per the Florida Statutes, that apply uniquely to each type of association.

For the purpose of the examination, please know these key proxy requirements as outlined here.

- **Condominiums and Co-Ops:**
    - General and limited proxies may be used to establish a quorum and are good for only 90 days after the date of first meeting for which it was given
    - Unit owners generally may not vote by general proxy
    - Proxies may not be used for electing the board
- **HOAs:**
    - To be considered as a valid proxy certificate, a proxy must be dated, must state the date, time, and place of the meeting for which it is given, and must be signed and dated by the authorized person executing the proxy
    - Proxies are good for only 90 days after the date of first meeting for which it was given
    - There is no restriction on using a proxy for elections

Voting and abstaining from voting

Voting and abstaining from voting is a right of each association member. Voting is a key to a fair and transparent management process, and represents the decisions of the majority of the voting members. In most cases, the vote can be decided by a majority of the votes cast. In the case of a tie, the motion is not carried and the vote fails.

There are several ways for voting to take place:

- General consent
- Voice vote
- Show of hands
- Roll call
- Ballot

Meeting Minutes and records requirements

Meeting Minutes are the official recording mechanism for capturing what was declared or voted upon in a meeting. Usually the minutes of the last meeting are provided as a reminder of what took place at the last gathering. Association managers should archive and publish the meeting minutes of all past meetings in a secure location and make them available for official inquiries as needed.

Remember these key points:

- When a majority vote is reached on something, it is recorded in the minutes and that makes it "official" for the members of the association to abide by
- The voting activity of all the directors are to be captured in the meetings
- The president votes last, so as to not influence any other participants
- The "minute books", or the full collection of past meeting minutes, are part of the official governing document body and must be properly stored and archived, with the same importance as bylaws, declarations, etc.

Election process, recall, and filling vacancies upon resignation

Association managers should be well familiar with the process for elections, recall, and subsequently, filling vacancies upon the resignation of board members or committee members.

- The officers and committee chairs are either elected or appointed. They are not usually elected by the members, but some associations may require the members to elect the officers in a voting session
- The meeting at which the officers are elected must be open to all of the members
- A majority vote of the directors is required to elect officers
- The election of the officers usually takes place at the organizational meeting held shortly after the annual owners' meeting
- The board may appoint officers rather than elect them, such as when the officers are not directors, as per the governing documents

- Vacancies are usually filled by appointment with election at the next meeting of the board of directors after the vacancy occurs.
- Because the directors elect the officers, they can vote to change officers at any time.

Quorum requirements

A "quorum" is the minimum amount of needed votes in order to fairly represent the collective voice of the voting body. If there are not enough members present to provide a valid quorum, then a vote cannot take place.

- There must be a valid quorum to have an official meeting and make decisions
- **Condominiums and cooperatives**: a quorum is a majority of the membership attending in person or by proxy, unless the bylaws specify a lower number. A condominium election may be held if 20% of the ballots are returned.
- **HOAs**: A quorum for a homeowners association is 30% unless a lower number is provided in the bylaws
- **Timeshares**: For timeshares, a quorum is 15% of the voting interests

Scope of authority of association officers and directors

It is important for community managers to understand the scope of authority of association officers and directors, and how they compare to a regular member. A regular member does not officially represent the association, rather, the association acts through its officers and agents. The board coordinates and votes on the association's policies and then the officers and agents carry out those policies.

In most cases, the Articles of Incorporation and By-laws documents will outline the structure of the officers of the association. If the documents do not set forth the officers, then each association must have at a minimum, a President, a Secretary and a Treasurer. The President and the Secretary must be two separate persons.

Board of Directors vs. Managers

It's important to understand the roles and relationship between the managers and the board. This is the guideline below:

- The Board of Directors sets forth policy for the association.
- Management carries out that policy.
- Management never sets policy.
- The Board of Directors never carries out that policy.

Notice content, posting, delivery requirements for board and association members

Association managers need to be familiar with the Notice content, posting, delivery requirements - and much of that has been covered thus far in this section of study guide. For the purposes of the examination, be very familiar with the table in the end of this section, and know the key points as illustrated, for each type of meeting.

Facilitate Committee Operations

Committees are special groups of members who are charged with handling a particular decision or point to research, such as creating a budget. They exist to assist the board, and provide data or information to the board. Committees are usually limited to fact-finding, information gathering, and making recommendations to the board. All meetings of committees or any other group assisting in association business are open meetings.

All Boards of Directors have the power to appoint committees. Usually the duties of the committees are set forth when they are appointed and it is usually in writing. The documents in some cases set forth the powers of the committees.

Key points to know:

- Meetings of a committee to take final action on behalf of the board or to make recommendations to the board regarding the association's budget must fully comply with the notice requirements for board meetings including notice or waiver of notice to committee members and posting of the notice at least 48 hours in advance of the meeting for the benefit of members.
- Meetings of committees that do not take final action on behalf of the board or do not make budget recommendations may be exempted from these requirements when the bylaws permit.
- In a nutshell, the **committee makes recommendations, not final decisions.**

Notice, agenda, and procedures for Committees

Notice, agenda, and procedures for Committees are prescribed in the founding documents or bylaws. Amendments, which are voted upon, can be added to the governing documents over time, to further define how committees are to operate within the operations of the association.

Budget Committees that make recommendations to the board regarding the association's annual budget must provide notice of their meetings 48 hours in advance and the meetings must be open to the unit owners to attend.

Voting certificates

A voting certificate is a document which specifies which owner, in the case of multiple-owners, who will be exercising their right to vote. For example, if a condominium unit is owned by 3 persons, this does not mean they get 3 votes. Rather, they must designate which one will vote using the Voting Certificate. This voting certificate becomes an official part of the records of the association. It designates the one person that can exercise the right to vote for a unit. When the unit is owned by more than one person (in most documents, married couples are considered one person), then the owners must get together and decide who can cast that one vote.

The last dated and properly executed voting certificate prevails, and they do not expire. In the case of a corporation owning a unit, the voting certificate must be signed by the president and attested to by the secretary.

Table: <u>Meeting Requirements</u> | *Summary of notice requirements and contents*

Meeting	Requirement		Florida Statutes	
	Condo/Co-Op	HOA	Condo/Co-Op	HOA
Board Meeting	Posted in a conspicuous place, Not less than **48 Hours**, with Agenda	Posted in a conspicuous place at least **48 Hours**	718.112	720.303
Budget Meeting	**14 Days** mailed, with Proposed Budget, and Posted	Pursuant to documents	718.112	720.303
Committee Meeting	Post at least **48 hours** in advance,	Post at least **48 hours** in advance, and indicate if architectural decisions will be made,	718.112	720.303
Annual Meeting	First Notice at **60 Days**; Then Second Notice is not less than **14 Days** mailed and Posted, With Agenda, and broadcast	Not less than **14 Days** mailed and Posted, and broadcast	718.112	720.306
Meeting to elect Directors of the Board, if not at the Annual Meeting	Posted at least **14 Days** in advance	Posted at least **14 Days** in advance	718.112	720.306
Emergency Meeting				

Meeting to discuss unit use changes or restrictions	**14 Days** mailed and Posted *Unless the docs require longer period*	**14 Days** mailed and Posted *Unless the docs require longer period*	718.112	720.303
Non-Emergency Assessments Meeting (Levy of Special Assessments)	Posted conspicuously at least **14 Days** in advance, and indicate that assessments will be decided upon	Posted conspicuously at least **14 Days** in advance, and indicate that assessments will be decided upon	718.112	720.303
Meetings with the Association's Attorney	Posted **48 Hours** in advance, *but meeting does not have to be open to members*	Posted **48 Hours** in advance, *but meeting does not have to be open to members*		

Part III - Budgets and Finance (25%)

This section covers 25% of the test material, so be sure to have a thorough understanding of the concepts and topics covered here. Reread this section as needed to have a competent understanding and familiarity with these knowledge points.

This section will cover Budgets, and other Finance topics. This is the topic outline of the exam-required knowledge points:

EXAM TOPICS FOR PART III - BUDGETS & FINANCE

1. Utilize Budget Procedures
    a. Knowledge of expenditure categories
    b. Knowledge of funding the budget
    c. Knowledge of budget adoption procedures
    d. Knowledge of reserve requirements
    e. Knowledge of amending the budget
    f. Knowledge of surplus funds

2. Budget for Reserves
    a. Knowledge of governing document existence
    b. Knowledge of reserves, waiver, and transfer procedures

3. Assist in Annual Financial Reporting
    a. Knowledge of reserve disclosures
    b. Knowledge of annual financial report and financial statement requirements

4. Knowledge of Control and Disbursement of Funds

5. Utilize Reserve Funds
    a. Knowledge of record keeping
    b. Knowledge of governing document existence
    c. Knowledge of appropriate use

6. Collect Assessments
    a. Knowledge of time and due dates of assessments
    b. Knowledge of developer obligation for assessments
    c. Knowledge of liability for assessments
    d. Knowledge of association assessment records
    e. Knowledge of procedures for levying assessments

Association Budgets

In its simplest form, a budget is a planned estimate of the operational expenses for the coming year. The "budget", which is usually a document that is published once a year, is how the association projects what revenues it will bring in and what expenses are anticipated to be paid in the upcoming year.It is usually based on the actual spending and expenditures of the previous years, and is formatted in a 12-month format.

The budget is the official mechanism by which the association discloses how much the members will need to pay in assessments in order to pay for the maintenance and other costs of running the association. It also provides how the members' assessments will be calculated. The budget is the primary tool that assists the board in estimating the amount of revenue that must be generated in order to pay the association's expenses.

The planned budget becomes the adopted reference point for calculating and allocating the unit owners' share of the funding needed to sustain the operations. When the budget is voted on and approved by the members, the funding amounts for the budgeted items are earmarked for future spending within the next coming year.

The expenses should be listed by account and classification and they must be scheduled on a monthly and an annual basis. **Common expenses** include the expenses of the operation, maintenance, repair, replacement, or protection of the common elements and association property. They also include the costs of carrying out the powers and duties of the association as well as reasonable transportation services, insurance for directors and officers, security, and bad debt, etc.

When declaring the finalized budget, a supplemental sheet explaining the basis for the line items is usually included. If there are limited common elements that are funded only by the units having use of them, a separate schedule must be provided for that limited common element.

Association boards have a fiduciary duty that is owed to all of the members of the association, and the budget assists the board in fulfilling this duty. Some associations create budget committees.

Committees that make recommendations to the board regarding the association budget must notice their meetings **48 hours in advance** and the meetings must be **open to the unit owners**. This is typically a once-a-year occurrence. The yearly budget is how the assessments (aka dues, fees or payments), that members must pay, will be calculated. Assessments are often collected annually, bi-annually, or quarterly (at least quarterly for condominiums).

Board members and managers refer to the budget frequently throughout the year, comparing monthly financial statements to the budget, to make certain that the association is operating within budget. If the association is "over" the budget limits, the board may consider making changes to the budget, but must follow the proper statutory procedures and the community's founding documents.
The budget process should begin up to three months in advance of the meeting where it is to be reviewed and approved.

The analysis should include any historical information that will be relevant to the upcoming year's budget:

- Contracts for maintenance
- Costs of utilities
- Example(s) of past budgets, ie - the previous year's approved budget document

Procedures for Calculating and Publishing the Budget

Budgets most commonly have two main categories of expenditure items, which are **operating** and **reserve**.

The operating section contains the expenses that relate to the day-to-day operation of the association. These expenses are referred to as "line items." These are the expenses that the association anticipates it will incur during the budget period for normal operation of the association, for example the electric bill or the cost of postage stamps.

The reserve portion of the budget, on the other hand, relates to funds restricted for specific purposes and usually involves large expenditures. **Florida condominium associations are required to establish reserves**, while homeowners associations' requirements are circumstantial and exemptible. Therefore, HOA's do not need to have reserves in their budgets unless there are specific circumstances that require it. In fact, the reality is many times the exact opposite - homeowners' associations' ability to establish reserves may be restricted by the association's governing documents themselves.

Once the budget document is finalized it is then put up to vote in the annual meeting to approve and pass the budget for the upcoming year. The document is typically mailed out or posted via the association website, for members to be able to reference it at any point throughout the year.

Categories of Expenditures

The budget document (or spreadsheet) will list the expense items as line items. These are the expenses that the association anticipates it will incur during the budget period for normal operation of the association.

The following is the list of expenditures expected to be included in the budget of a condominium association:

- Administration of the association
- Maintenance costs
- Rent for recreational and other commonly used facilities
- Taxes levied upon association property
- Property Management fees
- Taxes levied upon leased areas
- Insurance
- Security provisions
- Other expenses
- Operating capital
- Reserves
- Fees payable to the Florida real estate division

Funding the budget

The monies for the association budget is directly funded by the assessments collected by management from its members. For condominium associations, an assessment means a share of the funds which are required for the payment of common expenses, which from time to time is assessed against the unit owner.

The Homeowners' Act defines assessment as a sum or sums of money payable to the association, to the developer or other owner of common areas, or to recreational facilities and other properties serving the parcels by the owners of one or more parcels as authorized in the governing documents, which if not paid by the owner of a parcel, can result in a lien against the parcel.

How Assessments are calculated and funded

Owner assessments are calculated using a number of methods, including Allocation, Frequency, Total Units, Joint and Severable Liability for Assessment, Safe Harbor, etc. Although the method used can vary, the basic idea is that owners should EQUALLY be affected by the budget and have to pay for their fair share only. Therefore, the community manager must ensure that fair and equal practices are involved when calculating how the assessments are funded. Sometimes the predicament can be easily solved, for example - Painting a 100-Unit condo building will cost $5000, therefore the "Per Unit" cost is $50 per owner. Other times, it isnt as straightforward, such as a road paving project that only benefits a third of the residents.

For the purposes of the examination, make a note of the following as the most common methods of calculating assessments:

- **Allocation method**
- **Frequency**
- **Total Units**
- **Joint and Several Liability for Assessment**
- **Safe Harbor method**

Procedures for Adopting the Budget

The association documents will establish whether the budgets are adopted by the members as a whole, or by the Board of Directors. In most cases, the Board of Directors will set the budget for the next coming year.

Regardless of which method is used, the **notice for the meeting at which the budget is to be approved must be given to all owners**. They must be notified at least 14 days prior to the meeting. Notice must be delivered by postal mail or personal courier delivery (if using the mail method, this requires a receipt for receiving the notice as physical proof).

The association can then certify, by way of an affidavit document, that all were notified by mail or personal delivery. If the budget is to be approved by the Board of Directors, then the notice must give the time and place for the meeting and invite all owners to attend. The notice must include a copy of the proposed budget. Multi-phased condominiums must have separate budgets for each condominium and for the master association. When voting takes place, a quorum is required to consider the budget and a majority of the board members present is required to approve the budget.

The key points to remember for most associations are:

- **Proper notice for the meeting at which the budget is approved must be provided to all members**
- **14 Days Prior Notice - Is the legal guideline for providing this notice**
- **A copy of the proposed upcoming budget is to be included in the Notice.**

Condominiums require an additional step. Condominiums have specific budget adoption procedures that must be followed in order to lawfully pass the budget, above and beyond those mentioned above. The acceptance and passage of the condominium budget requires:

- **A meeting that is open to all unit owners,, with 14 days notice that includes a copy of the proposed budget, and is evidenced by executing an affidavit of mailing.**

Reserve requirements

Budget reserves, which provides for emergency funding for items like roofing or roadway repaving, is not only a good idea but is required in the case of Condominiums. This section will describe the reserve requirements as prescribed by Florida Statutes such as the Condo Act.

A separate budget must be made for the reserves for deferred maintenance and capital expense items.

The Condominium Act **requires** a reserve account for:

- **All items of capital expenditure or deferred maintenance greater than $10,000**
- **Roofing replacement**
- **Pavement resurfacing**
- **Building painting**
- **Any other item that the Board of Directors deems appropriate, and is properly voted upon**

In addition, in the case of condominiums only, proxies relating to the waiving or reducing the funding of reserves or using existing reserve funds for purposes other than those for which the reserves were intended shall contain the following statement in capitalized, bold letters in a font size larger than any other used on the face of the proxy:

"WAIVING OF RESERVES, IN WHOLE OR IN PART, OR ALLOWING ALTERNATIVE USES OF EXISTING RESERVES MAY RESULT IN UNIT OWNER LIABILITY FOR PAYMENT OF UNANTICIPATED SPECIAL ASSESSMENTS REGARDING THOSE ITEMS."

For HOA's the amount of the annual reserve account funding is facilitated in the same way as the central budget, and typically is included as part of those Notices and Meetings. The reserves must be funded in the same frequency as assessments are due from the owners, usually Annually. Any interest earned on the reserve funds must remain with the reserve fund. Reserve funds and operating funds must be calculated and tracked separately, and funds cannot be commingled.

The Reserve Budget should contain the following items, and be used only for their stated purpose:

- Beginning balance of each reserve item
- Amount added during the year
- Amount expended during the year
- Ending balance of each reserve item
- How reserves were estimated, date of estimation, policy of interest earned, whether reserves were waived or not
- Information on developer reserve accounts, if applicable

Amending the budget

Generally speaking, the same procedures and notice requirements that must be followed in order to adopt the budget must be followed in order to amend the budget. For condominiums, this would require:

- **A special meeting with notice delivered properly**
- **Included with the Notice , is a copy of the proposed budget at least 14 days prior to the date of the meeting.**

If the budget exceeds **115%** of the previous year's assessments, excluding reasonable reserves for repair or replacement, anticipated expenses which the Board does not expect to be incurred on a regular/annual basis, or betterments to the property, 10% of the voting members may petition the board to reconsider it.

The petition must be received within **21 days** of the adoption of the budget. The board must call a special meeting within 60 days to reconsider the budget. **At least 14 days notice must be given to the membership before the meeting to reconsider the budget**.

At the meeting, there must be a quorum of the owners present in order to approve the revised budget. If a quorum does not approve the new budget or if a quorum is not present, the originally submitted and approved budget remains the budget.

These are the key points to remember for Budget Amendments:

- **115% Rule:** If the budget exceeds 115% of the previous year's assessments, excluding reasonable reserves for repair or replacement, anticipated expenses which the Board does not expect to be incurred on a regular/annual basis, or betterments to the property,
- **Petition to Reconsider:** 10% of the voting members may petition the board to reconsider it.
- The petition must be received within 21 days of the adoption of the budget.
- **Special Meeting:** The board must call a special meeting within 60 days to reconsider the budget.
- At least **14 days notice** must be given to the membership before the meeting to reconsider the budget.
- **Quorum is needed:** At the meeting, there must be a quorum of the owners present in order to approve the revised budget.
- If a quorum does not approve the new budget or if a quorum is not present, the originally submitted and approved budget remains the budget.

Surplus funds

"Common surplus" means the amount of all receipts or revenues, including assessments, rents, or profits, collected by a condominium association which exceeds common expenses.

The amount of money left after deducting expenses from revenues is commonly called an operating/common surplus. Unit Owners have an undivided share in the common surplus. The rights to the common surplus remain in the association. Common surplus is owned by unit owners in the same shares as their ownership interest in the common
elements. **718.115 F.S.**

The provision of the Not-For-Profit Corporations Act requires that any surplus be used to reduce assessments. Chapter 617 F.S. However, common surplus resulting from a special assessment may either be returned to the unit owner or applied as a credit toward future assessments. **718.116 F.S.**

Annual Financial Reporting

The annual financial reporting for most community associations is prepared by a CPA, but the association manager or CAM will contribute to this process and provide them with the background information and supporting documentation.

Reserve Disclosures

Reserves must be disclosed and voted upon by members of the association in much the same way as the main budget is adopted and passed. Reserve funds should be used for the purposes stated in the budget. They should not be used for any other purposes without a vote of approval from the whole membership. In condominiums and cooperatives, a vote is required by law and must take place in advance of the expenditure of the funds.

Financial Reporting and Financial Statement Requirements

The Condominium Act says that within 90 days after the end of the fiscal year, or annually on a date provided in the bylaws, the association shall prepare and complete, or contract for the preparation and completion of, a financial report for the preceding fiscal year. Within 21 days after the final financial report is completed by the association or received from the third party, but not later than 120 days after the end of the fiscal year or other date as provided in the bylaws, the association shall mail to each unit owner at the address last furnished to the association by the unit owner, or hand deliver to each unit owner, a copy of the financial report or a notice that a copy of the financial report will be mailed or hand delivered to the unit owner, without charge, upon receipt of a written request from the unit owner.

An association shall prepare a complete set of financial statements in accordance with generally accepted accounting principles. (Commonly referred to as GAAP).

The financial statements must be based upon the association's total Annual Revenues, as follows:

- An association with total annual revenues of $150,000 or more, but less than $300,000, shall prepare **compiled** financial statements.

- An association with total annual revenues of at least $300,000, but less than $500,000, shall prepare **reviewed** financial statements.

- An association with total annual revenues of $500,000 or more shall prepare **audited** financial statements.

- An association with total annual revenues of less than $150,000 shall prepare a report of **cash receipts and expenditures**.

Avoid Commingling: Control and Disbursement of Funds

"Commingling" is the act of mixing funds set aside for one purpose with other funds set aside for a separate purpose, especially when it is necessary to keep the funds separate. Typically, this occurs when deposits and checks are thrown in together into the same bank account. It is important to keep these items separate. It is not always necessarily illegal or immoral, but it can lead to problems so it is best to avoid such situations.

All funds collected by a condominium association shall be maintained separately in the association's name. Reserve funds can be commingled with operating funds only for investment purposes.

Collecting Assessments

Assessments are the means by which the association operations and maintenance projects are funded. The declaration will set forth the formula for allocating the share of expenses and the schedule for payments, typically annually or quarterly.

Once the expenses are known for the upcoming year, and the income other than assessments and fines are subtracted, then the remainder is the total assessments required to meet the budget.

When the amount of assessments is determined for each unit, the Board of Directors must determine the payment schedule. In condominiums and cooperatives, the law requires that assessments be collected in advance and at least quarterly.

Under the condominium act, all owners must be assessed the same percentages as their ownership in the common elements. For cooperatives, the assessments are set forth in the documents. The percentage of ownership in the common elements is set by the developer at the time the community's founding documents are recorded.

Liability for assessments

Just like in a mortgage on your home, the property in a condominium serves as collateral for funds due. The owner is liable for all assessments coming due while he or she is the owner of the unit. When a condominium/lot is sold, the buyer becomes liable, jointly and severally, with the seller for all unpaid assessments for common expenses prior to the sale.

Liability for assessments cannot be waived by "waiver of the use" or the denial of enjoyment of either the unit or the common elements. If the documents so provide, and if an owner is delinquent, the assessments on that unit may be accelerated. Also, if the documents so provide, a delinquent owner can be denied the right to lease their unit.

If the documents provide for it, an interest may be charged on delinquent assessments. If not stated otherwise, 18% may be charged. Also, a late fee of $25.00 or 5% may be charged, whichever is greater.

Special Assessments

Special assessments may be required in order to provide funding for emergency or unplanned purposes. A need for a special assessment may arise when the expenses are more than anticipated, a reserve is more than anticipated, or the expense is earlier than anticipated. Unless the documents state otherwise, the Board of Directors can approve a special assessment.

To approve a Special Assessment:

- The Board must post a notice conspicuously and continuously for at least 14 days in advance of the meeting to consider a special assessment.
- They must also notify all owners at least 14 days in advance of the meeting to consider the special assessment and state the nature, estimated cost and a description of the special assessment.
- The Board must establish specific due dates for the assessment or the assessment installments.
- The Board must also identify the date at which the assessment is delinquent. The payment procedures should be in a resolution or in the minutes of the Board meeting.

The due date and the delinquent date should be provided clearly in the letter sent to all of the recipients of the special assessment notice. The notice to consider a special assessment is mailed to all of the owners with an explanation for the need for the additional funds. The notice will state the time, date, and place of meeting. Once the special assessment is approved, a second notice is sent out to all of the owners stating that the special assessment has been approved and setting forth the dates that payment(s) is due and the date that they are considered delinquent. The reason for the special assessment does not have to be stated in the second notice as it was stated already in the original notice.

Rental Collections

In a condominium or cooperative, the unit owner is ultimately liable for any delinquent assessments and fines, even if the unit is rented out. The association may make a written demand that the tenant pay to the association any rental payments to fulfill the monetary obligations of the unit owner in the event that a unit or parcel is occupied by a tenant and the unit owner is delinquent in paying any monetary obligation due to the association. The tenant must pay the monetary obligation to the association until the association has been paid in full and releases the tenant or the tenant discontinues tenancy of the unit. The association must mail written notice to the unit owner of the association's demand that the tenant make payments to the association. The association shall provide the tenant with written receipts for payments made.

A tenant who acts in good faith in response to a written demand from an association is immune from any claim from the unit owner.

- If the tenant prepaid rent to the unit owner before receiving the written demand from the association, the tenant shall receive credit for the prepaid rent for the applicable period and must make any subsequent rental payments to the association to be credited against the monetary obligations of the unit owner to the association.
- The tenant is not liable for increases in the amount of the monetary obligations due unless the tenant is notified in writing of the increase at least 10 days before the date the rent is due. The tenant shall be given a credit against rents due to the parcel owner in the amount of assessments paid to the Association
- An Association may evict a tenant who fails to pay a monetary obligation.
- The tenant does not, by virtue of payment of monetary obligations to the association, have any of the rights of a unit owner to vote in any election or to examine the books and records of the association.

Liens and Foreclosures

When a unit is sold to a new buyer, the unit owner is liable for all unpaid assessments that came due up to the time of transfer of title. This does not include an association that acquires title to a delinquent property through a foreclosure or deed-in-lieu. Therefore, the present parcel owner's liability for unpaid assessments is limited to any unpaid assessments that accrued before the association acquired title to the delinquent property.

An association can file for a lien on the unit for all unpaid assessments by having the association attorney file a "claim of lien" with the clerk of the county court.

A proper claim of lien must state:

- The legal description and owner of the property
- The name and address of the association
- The amount and date when the assessment became due
- It must be signed by an officer or agent of the association
- Must give written notice at least 45 days for homeowner associations and 30 days for condominium and cooperative associations prior to filing a claim of lien
- This written notice must be sent via registered/certified mail, return receipt requested and by first-class mail to the address listed in the association records and to the parcel address.

The claim of lien is effective from the time of its recording for a period of one year for condominiums and cooperatives, and five years for HOAs and timeshares. The procedure to foreclose on the lien is basically the same manner that one would on a mortgage. The board must give written notice of its intention to foreclose at least 30 days for condominiums and 45 days for homeowner associations in advance of filing the lawsuit. If this notice is not given then fees and costs cannot be legally recovered.

The first mortgage holder's liability for past due assessments is limited to the lesser of 1% of the original mortgage amount, or 12 months assessments.

Association Assets and Liabilities

Like most corporate entities, the association will have assets and liabilities. Assets are anything owned that has monetary value. Liabilities are items or monies which are owed to others.

Association **assets** typically include:

- Bank accounts
- Petty cash
- Investments
- Assessments owed the association (accounts receivable)
- Furniture, fixtures and equipment
- Real property
- Utility deposits
- Prepaid expenses (insurance premiums)

Association **liabilities** typically include:

- Invoices not yet paid (accounts payable)
- Assessment fees received before their due date (unearned/prepaid assessments)
- Long term debt
- Deferred revenue
- Reserve obligations

On a balance sheet the total **fund balance** is the difference between the assets and liabilities. Also known as equity, it shows the worth of the association at a given date.

Accounts Receivable Records for Condominiums

The Board of Directors must keep a separate account for each unit of the condominium of the assessments due and collected. The accounts are a part of the permanent records of the condominium and should state the name and address of the owners of the unit, the amount of each assessment, the date it came due, the amounts paid and the balance which remains unpaid. This list should be filed by unit number not by owners name. Owners are jointly and severally liable for assessments due on a unit when ownership changes.

Observe the following for condominiums:

- In condominiums and cooperatives the Board must be prepared to deliver a certificate stating the status of all assessments affecting a unit within 15 days after a request by an owner or mortgage holder.
- Any person including the mortgage holder or purchaser, but not the owner, may rely on the certificate and is protected by its content and may presume it to be accurate.

Annual Fees

All corporations in Florida must file an Annual Report with the Department of State. In addition to that requirement, all condominiums and cooperatives must file a copy of their annual report by January 1st with the Division of Florida Condominiums, Timeshares, and Mobile Homes for the purpose of remitting and annual fee required by the statutes.

The guidelines for the Annual Fee are:

- This fee is $4.00 for each unit.
- If the fee is not paid by March 1, then a 10% penalty can be assessed and the association is prohibited from maintaining or defending any action in the courts.
- When paying the annual fee the association must provide a permanent mailing address.
- A post office box is acceptable. A management company address for the association address is not acceptable.

A timeshare must remit $2.00 for each seven days of "annual use availability" in each time share unit within the time share plan.

HOA Reporting to DBPR

As of 2013, Every CAM, or the association when there is no CAM, shall report to DBPR by November 22, 2013, the name of the association, the FEIN number, mailing and physical address, the number of parcels, and the total amount of revenues and expenses from the annual budget of the association.

Part IV - Insurance (12%)

This section will cover the Insurance content and is approximately 12% of the scope of the test questions. Of all the five sections of content, this is the smallest component. Please don't take it lightly though, as there are several critical points to remember here.

There are several moments in time each year when the community association, or the CAM, must deal with the topic of insurance. Insurance by definition is the practice or arrangement by which a company or government agency provides a guarantee of paid compensation in the event of a specific loss, damage, illness, or death; in return, the agency receives the payment of a premium.

Insurance provides protection against unexpected mishaps and accidents, and the community association will have to ensure that it is protected against these unfortunate events.

EXAM TOPICS FOR PART IV - INSURANCE

1. Obtain and Fulfill Insurance Requirements
    a. Knowledge of association property and liability insurance
    b. Knowledge of unit owner property and liability insurance
    c. Knowledge of limited liability and exclusions
    d. Knowledge of flood insurance
    e. Knowledge of loss control procedures
    f. Knowledge of insurance policy deductibles
    g. Knowledge of governing documents
    h. Knowledge of Certificates of Insurance
    i. Knowledge of handling insurance claims
    j. Knowledge of fidelity bonding
    k. Knowledge of performance bonds
    l. Knowledge of Florida Windstorm Underwriting Association

2. Obtain Insurance Coverage on Officers and Directors
    a. Knowledge of liability insurance coverage for officers and directors
    b. Knowledge of liability insurance exclusions for officers and directors

Insurance Requirements for Associations

One of the key responsibilities of the board is to insure the common property of the association and provide for protections to be in place in the event of an accident or mishap. As a community manager it is critical to understand the insurance requirements of the various types of communities. For most communities the insurance requirements are dictated by either statutory law, or it is a specific item covered in the community's founding documents. Most important to note is, **F.S. Chapter 718 makes it a requirement for condominiums in particular have insurance**.

The board must have a clear understanding of the statutory requirements and the requirements set forth in the community's documents. In Florida, insurance laws for communities are defined and regulated by the Departed of Financial Services and the Office of Insurance, which is part of the Office of the CFO (Chief Financial Officer).

Due to the myriad of complexities involved in this area, for the purposes of the licensing examination only a general familiarity and fundamental knowledge is required. There are insurance agencies that specialize in community association insurance, and it is highly recommended that associations consult an attorney or insurance expert regarding which coverage to purchase.

The types of insurance that a community association commonly deals with is **Property Insurance, Liability Insurance, Directors & Officers Insurance (D&O), Flood insurance,** and **Workers Comp** coverage.

The association is responsible for:

Property insurance, also referred to as hazard insurance, protects against accidents and events to the property, most importantly the common areas which are co-owned by all the members. Property insurance protects the common elements against losses resulting from natural and manmade events, such as hail/storm damage; or damage to property resulting from the actions of a third party, such as an act of vandalism which has damaged some parts of the common areas.

Liability Insurance is used to protect the association in the event that someone sues, most likely for making claims that an injury has resulted due to the negligence of the association.

Condominium Owners' Responsibility for Unit-Level Insurance

For condominium owners there is an additional requirement for insurance that is very important. In addition to the property insurance that the association procures for the common elements, the individual unit owners also purchase property insurance for items which are excluded.

Unit Owner Property insurance covers the items which are excluded from the association's policy, and these items have been defined in F.S 718.

These exclusions are:

"All personal property within the unit or limited common elements, and floor, wall, and ceiling coverings, electrical fixtures, appliances, water heaters, water filters, built-in cabinets and countertops, and window treatments, including curtains, drapes, blinds, hardware, and similar window treatment components, or replacements of any of the foregoing which are located within the boundaries of the unit and serve only such unit. Such property and any insurance thereupon is the responsibility of the unit owner."
718.111 F.S.

Special Exception for Owner Conduct Issues

There are certain circumstances where an individual unit owner may be liable for damages caused to the common elements as a result of negligence on the part of the owner. To address these situations there is an exception to the rule, in cases where the owner's conduct is at fault and the incident could have been avoided.

For example, if the individual unit owner accidentally causes damage to the pool pump, elevator or other community facility as a result of negligence.

<u>Chapter 718 of the Florida Statutes defines this as follows:</u>

"A unit owner is responsible for the costs of repair or replacement of any portion of the condominium property not paid by insurance proceeds if such damage is caused by intentional conduct, negligence, or failure to comply with the terms of the declaration or the rules of the association by a unit owner, the members of his or her family, unit occupants, tenants, guests, or invitees, without compromise of the subrogation rights of the insurer. Similarly, a unit owner is responsible for damage done to other unit owners' property, real or personal,

when such damage is caused by intentional conduct, negligence, or failure to comply with the terms of the declaration or the rules of the association by a unit owner, the members of his or her family, unit occupants, tenants, guests, or invitees, without compromise of the subrogation rights of the insurer."
718.111 F.S.

Limited Liability and Exclusions

There may be an incident where someone successfully sues the association, and each individual owner may be liable for a portion of the damages won. There are some provisions in place to ensure that the owner is protected from facing an unreasonable or disproportionate share of the liability.

Chapter 718 provides for the following:

"The liability of the owner of a unit for common expenses is limited to the amounts for which he or she is assessed for common expenses from time to time in accordance with chapter 718, the declaration, and bylaws. The owner of a unit may be personally liable for the acts or omissions of the association in relation to the use of the common elements, but only to the extent of his or her pro rata share of that liability in the same percentage as his or her interest in the common elements, and then in no case shall that liability exceed the value of his or her unit. In any legal action in which the association may be exposed to liability in excess of insurance coverage protecting it and the unit owners, the association shall give notice of the exposure within a reasonable time to all unit owners, and they shall
have the right to intervene and defend."
718.119 F.S.

Unfortunately, lawsuits and judgements against the association as a whole do happen, and each individual owner may be liable for a portion of the damages won. Thankfully these provisions are there to ensure that the owner is protected from facing an unreasonable or disproportionate share of the liability.

D&O Insurance - Liability Protection for Directors and Officers

There is a specific insurance policy type that can protect against accidental behavior or mishaps on the part of the board members. Although it is not meant to directly indemnify the covered party in the event of a claim, rather it works to provide a benefit to offset legal costs for the lawsuit. Usually called a claim of "breach of duty", there may be an instance where the lawsuit is presented. D&O essentially is there to provide reimbursement for legal costs.

Directors & Officers liability Insurance (often called "D&O") is a form of liability insurance that is payable to the directors and officers of a company, or to the organization itself, as reimbursement for losses or advancement of defense costs, in the event an insured suffers such a loss as a result of a legal action brought for alleged wrongful acts in their capacity as directors and officers.

There are two types of D&O insurance, known as "Claims Made" or "Occurrence", and this is to address the timing of the claim being made. In the claims made method the association is protected against any covered incident that "occurs" during the policy period, regardless of when a claim is filed. Claims made to the insurance company after the coverage period ends will not be covered, even if the alleged incident occurred while the policy was in force. In the occurrence method the policy addresses the claims as they come in, even after the policy
has been canceled, as long as the incident occurred during the time period in which The coverage was in force. An occurrence policy offers permanent coverage for incidents that occur during the policy period.

Of course, this coverage does not apply in the event of intentionally illegal or malicious acts. In the event of an investigation of the association or incident, legal costs resulting from this can be reimbursed in some cases, as part of a D&O policy. The concept of fidelity bonding, a means of protection in the event of malicious or fraudulent activity, is discussed later in this chapter

Worker's Comp

Workers' compensation insurance, referred to commonly as "Workers Comp", is a form of insurance providing wage-replacement and medical benefits to employees injured in the course of employment in exchange for mandatory relinquishment of the employee's right to sue their employer for the tort of negligence.

As this may not apply in all situations, for example if the community association does not employ any staff, it is only mentioned briefly for the purposes of the examination. However it is important to be aware of this point, and that in the event that the community is large and has any operational or maintenance staff to run it, there may be a requirement to obtain Workers Comp insurance. As this is a cost to the association, it would be an item that is included in the annual budget and is funded by the members.

Flood Insurance

As you might expect, flood insurance protects against property loss from water or liquid flooding. To determine risk factors for specific properties, insurers will often refer to topographical maps that depict where the low-lying areas which might be prone to flooding are located.

To facilitate this, Congress created the National Flood Insurance Program (NFIP) in 1968. This program is administered by the Federal Emergency Management Agency (FEMA) to help provide a means for property owners to financially protect themselves in the event of a flood incident.

If the community participates in the program, the NFIP offers flood insurance to homeowners, renters, and business owners in that community. Participating communities agree to adopt and enforce ordinances, such as minimum elevation requirements for new homes and buildings, which meet or exceed FEMA requirements, in order to reduce the risk impacts of flooding.

In areas which are deemed to be at higher risk, Congress has mandated federally regulated lenders to require flood insurance on properties that are located in areas prone to flooding.

Loss Control Procedures

Loss control, or loss prevention, refers to any measures or safeguards which are in place and designed to eliminate or reduce occurrences that could result in injury, death, financial loss, damage, or loss of physical property. An example of a loss control mechanism would be a preventative maintenance program that ensures certain equipment is kept in running order.

Insurance companies will not pay for damages that results from something the board may have knowledge of but did not remedy the situation. For example, if the association had knowledge that a pool was not balanced properly and the chemicals could cause skin irritation or burning, but the association did not take measures to remedy the problem as an effective method of loss control, the insurance company will not cover the damages owed to injured swimmers. As a community manager, it is critical to stay abreast of any maintenance needs and always be proactive to reduce the risk of issues or injuries.

Insurance Policy Deductibles

In an insurance policy, the deductible is the amount paid out of pocket by the policy holder before an insurance provider will pay any expenses. We are usually familiar with this example with regards to our automobile insurance policies. For example, in the event of a collision the first $500 spent on expenses for the repair is paid by the policy holder and is commonly known as the deductible. Deductibles for property and liability insurance work in much the same way. As this can be an item that in included in the association budget, it must be identified and communicated to all the members, and is to be voted in as part of the annual budget voting.

Condominium insurance policies may include deductibles as determined by the board:

> "1. The deductible amount must be consistent with common standard practices for communities of similar size and age, and having similar construction and facilities in the area where the condominium property is located.
>
> 2. The deductible may be based upon available funds, including reserve accounts, or predetermined assessment authority at the time the insurance is obtained.
>
> 3. The board shall establish the amount of deductibles based upon the level of available funds and predetermined assessment authority at a meeting of the board."

Fidelity Bonds

Earlier in the text we explored how D&O insurance coverage can protect in the event of accidental errors or omissions made by the directors or officers of the association without a malicious intent. But what happens if there is a case of intentional fraud or malfeasance?

Fidelity bonding protects the association in case of loss as a result of fraudulent or illegal activity on the part of any staff, employee, board member, or president. The requirement for a fidelity bond was essentially put in place to address the issue of stealing from the association's coffers.

The amount of the bond is equal to the total amount that the criminal could potentially steal. In lieu of a fidelity bond, an insurance policy that can provide a comparable level of loss protection may be adequate.

This is covered in Florida Statutes Chapters 718 and 720 as follows:

> "The insurance policy or fidelity bond must cover the maximum funds that will be in the custody of the association or its management agent at any one time."
> **720.3033 F.S. & 718.111 F.S.**

Performance Bond

Performance bonds are a device used by contractors to ensure that they will complete the work they have promised. A performance bond is a surety bond issued by an insurance company to guarantee satisfactory completion of a project by a contractor. The Performance Bond secures the contractor's promise to perform the contract in accordance with its terms and conditions, at the agreed upon price that was quoted, and that the work was done within the time allowed.

It is very common to require that any bidding contractors be licensed to operate, pull permits when needed, and provide a performance bond to guarantee the successful delivery of the project. Requirements like these will filter out any non-competent or unlawful contractors from the bidding process.

Another less common bond that contractors will provide is the labor-and-material payment bond. The labor-and-material payment bonds are usually issued alongside the performance bonds, and the aim is to cover a contractor's failure to pay labor, materials, or other obligations. These bonds are intended to defend against any lawsuits or claims against the association as a result of a contractor's failure.

Citizens Property Insurance Company (CPIC)

Citizens Property Insurance Corporation (CPIC) is a not-for-profit, tax-exempt government corporation established to provide insurance protection to Florida property owners. It is commonly referred to as "Citizen's" insurance. CPIC currently provides coverage to hundreds of thousands of homes, businesses, and condominiums in Florida. Citizens offers several types of coverage for business owners, homeowner associations and condominium building owners who cannot find coverage in the private market, and also meet Citizens' criteria for underwriting eligibility.

Florida Windstorm Underwriting Association (FWUA)

The Florida Windstorm Underwriting Association (FWUA) was formed in the 1990's following the devastation of Hurricane Andrew to the south Florida region. It is the predecessor to the CPIC. These organizations are established to provide protection to Florida homeowners who might have coverage denied elsewhere via traditional insurers.

Part V - Management/Maintenance (18%)

This section will cover Management and Maintenance topics for the examination. The material in this section makes up approximately 18% of the scope of the test questions. This is not a majority component, but nonetheless the topics presented here are thought of as the most important tasks that a community association manager does.

The association, or the subcontracted CAM firm, provides the official coordination and oversight of the maintenance and repair needs of the community. We often consider that the maintenance and upkeep of the community's common area elements as one of the major responsibilities of the board. This includes identifying property that needs to be maintained, seeking competitive bids for maintenance, scheduling and coordinating the completion of maintenance projects, and paying the vendors that are hired to perform the services. Therefore it is critical for a competent CAM to have a fundamental understanding and working knowledge of these topics.

EXAM TOPICS FOR PART V - MANAGEMENT & MAINTENANCE

1. Enforce Governing Documents
    a. Knowledge of rights and obligations of tenants/owners
    b. Knowledge of violations and enforcement procedures
    c. Knowledge of procedures for imposing fines, penalties, and fees
    d. Knowledge of alternative dispute resolution

2. Facilitate Agreements and Leases
    a. Knowledge of bidding requirements
    b. Knowledge of contract requirements
    c. Knowledge of governing document existence

3. Repair and Maintain Property
    a. Knowledge of pool maintenance requirements
    b. Knowledge of security guard requirements
    c. Knowledge of pest control regulatory requirements
    d. Knowledge of elevator service and operation requirements
    e. Knowledge of property maintenance requirements

Enforcing the Governing Documents

The oversight of the maintenance of the community's common elements is a primary role of the association. However, this is only half of the upkeep effort. The association, or CAM manager firm, is responsible for inspecting the property of the association's members to ensure that individual homeowners are complying with their responsibilities, as set forth in the community's declaration of covenants.

The community's governing documents are where the responsibilities of the individual home owners are detailed. The declaration of covenants of the homeowners' association often contain regulations on architectural matters, exterior appearance, and the responsibilities of the homeowner to maintain their property,

In addition to homeowner responsibilities, there is also a section that defines the association's responsibility to maintain the common elements, roadways or easements. Thus, the community association has the double duty of enforcing and managing both domains - the common areas and the unit owners' properties. The declaration of covenants, or statutory law at times, provides us with guidelines for enforcing these violations, the rights of tenants, the proper procedure for levying fines, and ways to resolve disputes.

Rights and Obligations of Owners/Tenants

Covenants, Conditions, and Restrictions (CCRs) are the rules and regulations set forth in the governing documents, which declare these rules which must be followed. The CCR's are essentially, the "**deed restrictions**" that the homeowners must adhere to when living in that community. The enforcement level of CCRs can vary from one community to another, with some associations not doing very much to inspect or enforce any violations. This can be due to time or funding constraints, or an intentional decision so as to not create disharmony in the community.

Violations and enforcement procedures

The association may impose fines, or suspend for a reasonable period of time, the right of the unit owner to use the common elements, common facilities or any other association property for failure to comply with any provision of the declaration, bylaws or reasonable rules.

However, the association may not impair the right of the owner or tenant to have vehicular and pedestrian ingress or egress from the parcel, including, but not limited to, the right to park. A fine may be levied on the basis of each day of a continuing violation with a single notice for a hearing.

- The fine may not exceed $100 per violation or $1,000 in the aggregate. A fine may not become a lien against a condominium unit or owner. For HOAs, fines less than $1,000 may not become a lien against the lot or Owner.
- A fine or suspension may not be imposed unless the Association first provides at least 14 days' written notice and an opportunity for a hearing to the unit owner or his guests/tenants.
- For condominiums, the hearing must be held before a committee of other unit owners who are neither board members nor persons residing in a board member's household.

Procedures for imposing fines, penalties, and fees

Fines are imposed typically by a committee that has been charged with identifying and processing any violations. For HOAs, the hearing committee must be three members who are not directors, officers, association employees, or the spouse, parent, child, brother or sister of a director, officer or employee.

For condominiums, members of the hearing committee cannot also be members of the board of directors. If the committee does not come to a valid and compliant agreement, the fine or suspension in question may not be imposed.

For HOAs, if a fine or suspension is imposed, the association must provide written notice of such fine or suspension by mail or hand delivery to the parcel owner and, if applicable, to any tenant, licensee, or invited guests of the parcel owner.

If an owner is more than 90 days delinquent in paying a monetary obligation due to the association, the association may suspend the right of the unit owner or the owner's occupant to use the common elements, common facilities, or any other association property until the monetary obligation is paid in full.

These are the exceptions:

- Limited common elements intended for use by that unit only
- Common elements needed to access the unit
- Utility services provided to the unit
- Parking spaces or elevators

Methods of alternative dispute resolution

The common methods of resolving disputes outside of the courts is arbitration or mediation. Alternative dispute resolution procedures can be initiated by the parties or may be compelled by legislation, the courts, or contractual terms.

Arbitration - This is a form of alternative dispute resolution used as a way to settle matters outside of the courts. The dispute will be decided by one or more persons, which renders the "arbitration award" to the winner. An arbitration award is legally binding on both sides and enforceable in the courts.

Mediation - Another form of alternative dispute resolution in which a third party negotiates an agreement between the parties in conflict. Unlike arbitration, mediation does not involve a final, decision-making judgement by the third party. Rather, they facilitate the negotiations to come to an agreement directly.

Facilitating Agreements and Leases

At times the association will need to coordinate and manage bidding for contractors, or the leasing of certain common area elements. It is important that associations and CAM firms follow the guidelines for soliciting and accepting bids, and executing contracts with the providers of those services. These providers are usually construction contractors, landscapers, pool and equipment servicers, elevator maintenance contractors, pest control operators, etc.

Bidding and Contracting Requirements

Contracting a provider to perform some kind of work, and transactions between an association and any of its directors or any corporation or entity in which a director has an interest, must be approved by two-thirds of the directors of the association and entered into the minutes of the meeting. At the next owner meeting, this contract must be disclosed to the members who also have the right to cancel the contract with a majority vote.

Condos and Co-ops with more than 10 units must obtain competitive bids if the contract exceeds 5% of the association's total annual budget including reserves. Condos or co-ops with 10 or less units may opt out of this requirement if approved by two-thirds of the owners.

The association is not required to accept the lowest bid. It is not always the best choice to go by price alone. If a contract for the purchase, lease, or renting of materials or equipment, or for the provision of services, requires payment by an HOA that exceeds 10 percent of the budget, including reserves, the HOA must get competitive bids. However, the HOA is not required to accept the lowest bid. Competitive bids are not required if the business entity with which the Association desires to enter into a contract is the only source of supply for that service.

Items Required in a Contract

Community associations who contract with a provider to perform a service should require the following items on all contracts:

- Bid Specifications
- Certificate(s) of Insurance
- Description
- Performance Bond
- Copies of Licensure or Credentials
- Building or Coding Permits as required by the project
- Notice of Commencement
- Warranty/Guarantees of Work Quality; also include Manufacturer's Warranty for materials, ie - Roofing materials
- Release of Lien/Lien Clause

Repairs and Maintenance for the Property

Community association managers and board members should be familiar with the fundamental legal requirements for certain maintenance matters such as elevators and swimming pools. This section will explore the guidelines for security guards, pool maintenance, pest control/fumigation, and elevator operations.

Pool maintenance requirements

Communities with swimming pools must adhere to pool maintenance requirements as regulated by the state. The Department of Health, Division of Environmental Health and the County Health Departments oversee swimming pools in the State of Florida.

Key points to know for the examination:

- All pools initially must submit plans to the department before they will issue a building permit. The pool will be inspected by the department, and then an operating permit will be issued.
- Licenses for public pools must be renewed each year and will be inspected before the renewal permit is issued. They will be inspected periodically during the year. The renewal will be prior to July 1 and the fee must be paid no later than June 15 each year.
- The quality of the water will be monitored closely from the water supplied by the local utility to the maintenance of the water quality by the association.
- All pools must be lit if they are to be used at night (defined as one half hour before sunset to one half hour after sunrise) and the lighting must provide adequate light so that all portions of the bottom are visible without glare.
- Pools with heaters shall have a maximum water temperature of 104 degrees F. Pools of 200 square feet or greater shall have "NO DIVING", in four inch letters included on the rules.
- Showers must be readily available and all bathers must shower before entering the pool. The bathing load must be posted as well as the hours of operation.
- If attendants are present, they must be first aid and lifesaving qualified.

- In a minimum of 1" letters, the following rules must be posted and legible from the pool deck: The pool deck is defined as within four feet of the pool curb.
    a. No food, drink, glass or animals in pool or pool deck.

b. No glass or animals in fenced pool area (or 50 feet from unfenced pool).
c. Bathing Load: _____persons.
d. Pool hours: _____a.m. to _____p.m.
e. Shower before entering
f. For new or modified pools submitted for plan approval application on or after the effective date of this rule, their posted sign shall add: <u>Do not swallow the pool water.</u>

Security guard requirements

Security guard requirements are defined in Chapter 493 of the Florida Statutes. Community associations who contract with a security provider will need to be compliant with any Chapter 493 rules. The Department of Agriculture and Consumer Services regulates the security profession and has authority over both licensed and unlicensed persons and business engaged in private security activities.

Important points to know:

- Any security officers hired through a security agency must have a Class D license as well as the security agency. A board should be assured that any security agency that they are considering for a contract has the proper licenses.
(Copies of the licenses should be attached to any contract proposal.)
- Associations that hire unarmed guards as employees of the association must be sure that the guards are registered with the State of Florida. Licensure is not required. Registration is required.
(This class of guards is known as proprietary security guards. Licensed security guards and registered proprietary officers are not law enforcement officers and do not have police powers regarding arrest or use of force.)
- Licensed security guards must be in uniform while performing their duties and must have at least one patch on their uniform that identifies the licensed agency for which they work. They must also have an identification card in their possession.
- Only security officers with both Class D and G licenses may carry firearms.

Pest control regulatory requirements

Pest control regulatory requirements for community associations are defined in Florida Statutes Chapter 482. The Department of Agriculture and Consumer Services controls the licensing and operations rules for the pest control industry.
If the community association plans to do it in-house, it is okay to spray the grounds but it is not acceptable to fumigate. It is also all right for the owner of a unit to spray their own unit. But, if it is someone other than the owner, that person must be licensed by the state.
Therefore, association employees may perform pest control in the common areas only, but not in an owner's unit. Fumigation is to gas-bomb a unit with aerosol sprays. If the association plans to fumigate then it must have a license, whether it be the common elements or in a private unit.

Elevator service and operation requirements

It is important for community managers and board members to be familiar with the elevator service and operation requirements in Florida. If a community in the state operates an elevator on the premises it must comply with State Codes regarding the operation and regular maintenance of an elevator. The elevator owner is legally responsible for the safe operation, proper maintenance, and inspection and correction of code deficiencies of the elevator.

Important requirements to know for the examination:

- The elevator must be ready for the handicapped. It must have a support rail on at least one wall and no rough edges.
- The certificate of operation must be posted in a conspicuous location on the elevator and must be framed with a transparent cover. The certificate of operation must state "**No Smoking**".
- The Division has the authority to suspend the operation of an elevator for safety reasons.
- If an elevator accident occurs and someone is hurt or killed, you must file a report of that accident within five days on their form. The fine for not reporting is up to $1000.
- Each building of six stories or more in height must be keyed to operate in fire emergency situations with one master key.

Property maintenance requirements

The association is responsible for maintaining the common property of the association, such as the entrance gates, roadways or the community pool. The Specific common property items are defined in the founding documents.

The Board of Directors is responsible for contracting someone to take care and maintain the property for the association. When the board fails to properly perform their duties, an individual owner has the right to act against the board for failure to do so. If an individual owner intentionally or negligently damages the common property, the association has the right to bring an action against the owner to recover damages.

Test Topics - Full Outline

This is a compact review of the core concepts for the examination. You can print these following pages in this section to have on hand for a quick-reference during your studies. Please remember though, reference materials are not allowed inside the test center during the examination process.

EXAM TOPICS FOR PART I - LAW

1. Utilize the Not-for-Profit Corporate Act (Chapter 617, F.S.)
    a. Knowledge of the scope of authority of a not-for profit corporation

2. Utilize the Condominium Act (Chapter 718, F.S. and F.A.C.)
    a. Knowledge of ownership of and additional alterations to common elements
    b. Knowledge of governing document existence
    c. Knowledge of disclosure requirements
    d. Knowledge of rights, privileges, and obligations of the unit owner

3. Utilize the Florida Vacation Plan and Timesharing Act (Chapter 721, F.S.)
    a. Knowledge of record keeping and financial reporting requirements
    b. Knowledge of differences between timeshare and other forms of regulated property ownership

4. Utilize the Fair Housing Act and Americans with Disability Act
    a. Knowledge of protected categories
    b. Knowledge of familial status provisions
    c. Knowledge of physical handicap provisions
    d. Knowledge of exemption options

5. Utilize the Cooperative Act (Chapter 719, F.S. and F.A.C.)
    a. Knowledge of governing document existence
    b. Knowledge of rights, privileges, and obligations of the developer
    c. Knowledge of transition requirements

6. Utilize the Homeowners' Association Act (Chapter 720, F.S. and F.A.C.)

7. Utilize Towing Statute (Chapter 715.07, F.S.)

8. Knowledge of Association's Right of Access to Individual Units

    a. Knowledge of governing document existence

    b. Knowledge of differences among common elements, limited common elements, common areas, and association property

    c. Knowledge of cable television requirements

9. Utilize Lien Laws

    a. Knowledge of statutory and documentary assessment lien rights

    b. Knowledge of statutory and documentary construction lien rights

    c. Community Association Management, Part VIII, Chapter 468, F.S. and Chapter 61-20, F.A.C.

EXAM TOPICS FOR PART II - PROCEDURES (NOTICING, AND CONDUCTING MEETINGS)

1. Notice procedures for the Association and Board Meetings

    a. Knowledge of types of meetings

    b. Knowledge of requirements of conducting a meeting (Association membership and special meetings, and meetings of the Board)

    c. Knowledge of proof of notice of meeting

    d. Knowledge of agenda requirements

    e. Knowledge of proxy requirements

    f. Knowledge of voting and abstaining from voting

    g. Knowledge of minutes and records requirements

    h. Knowledge of election process, recall, and filling vacancies upon resignation

    i. Knowledge of quorum requirements

    j. Knowledge of scope of authority of association officers and directors

    k. Knowledge of notice content, posting, delivery requirements for board and association members

2. Facilitate Committee Operations

    a. Knowledge of creation of committees

    b. Knowledge of scope of authority

    c. Knowledge of notice, agenda, and procedures

    d. Knowledge of development and understanding of committee reports

    e. Knowledge of search committee functions

3. Knowledge of Voting Procedures

    a. Knowledge of governing document existence

    b. Knowledge of balloting

    c. Knowledge of developer rights and privileges

    d. Knowledge of transition members' meeting

    e. Knowledge of eligibility requirements

    f. Knowledge of voting certificates

EXAM TOPICS FOR PART III - BUDGETS

1. Utilize Budget Procedures
    a. Knowledge of expenditure categories
    b. Knowledge of funding the budget
    c. Knowledge of budget adoption procedures
    d. Knowledge of reserve requirements
    e. Knowledge of amending the budget
    f. Knowledge of surplus funds

2. Budget for Reserves
    a. Knowledge of governing document existence
    b. Knowledge of reserves, waiver, and transfer procedures

3. Assist in Annual Financial Reporting
    a. Knowledge of reserve disclosures
    b. Knowledge of annual financial report and financial statement requirements

4. Knowledge of Control and Disbursement of Funds

5. Utilize Reserve Funds
    a. Knowledge of record keeping
    b. Knowledge of governing document existence
    c. Knowledge of appropriate use

6. Collect Assessments
    a. Knowledge of time and due dates of assessments
    b. Knowledge of developer obligation for assessments
    c. Knowledge of liability for assessments
    d. Knowledge of association assessment records
    e. Knowledge of procedures for levying assessments

EXAM TOPICS FOR PART IV - INSURANCE

1. Obtain and Fulfill Insurance Requirements
    a. Knowledge of association property and liability insurance
    b. Knowledge of unit owner property and liability insurance
    c. Knowledge of limited liability and exclusions
    d. Knowledge of flood insurance
    e. Knowledge of loss control procedures
    f. Knowledge of insurance policy deductibles
    g. Knowledge of governing documents
    h. Knowledge of Certificates of Insurance
    i. Knowledge of handling insurance claims
    j. Knowledge of fidelity bonding

  k. Knowledge of performance bonds
  l. Knowledge of Florida Windstorm Underwriting Association
2. Obtain Insurance Coverage on Officers and Directors
  a. Knowledge of liability insurance coverage for officers and directors
  b. Knowledge of liability insurance exclusions for officers and directors

EXAM TOPICS FOR PART V - MAINTENANCE

1. Enforce Governing Documents
  a. Knowledge of rights and obligations of tenants/owners
  b. Knowledge of violations and enforcement procedures
  c. Knowledge of procedures for imposing fines, penalties, and fees
  d. Knowledge of alternative dispute resolution
2. Facilitate Agreements and Leases
  a. Knowledge of bidding requirements
  b. Knowledge of contract requirements
  c. Knowledge of governing document existence
3. Repair and Maintain Property
  a. Knowledge of pool maintenance requirements
  b. Knowledge of security guard requirements
  c. Knowledge of pest control regulatory requirements
  d. Knowledge of elevator service and operation requirements
  e. Knowledge of property maintenance requirements

Sample Exam Prep Questions

Example test questions are provided below. They are formatted in the style and spirit of the actual examination questions. The state test will have 100 Multiple-Choice questions, similar in structure to the ones presented here. For each question, the correct answer is shown in **boldface type**.

1. The Association must provide _____ notice in advance of a meeting where the budget is voted on and approved.
    a. 10 Days
    b. 7 Days
    c. 14 Days
    d. 1 Month (30 Days)

2. Chapter 719 of the Florida Statutes is also known as the _____ Act.
    a. Fair Housing
    b. Cooperative
    c. Homeowners Association
    d. Equal Rights

3. Homeowners Associations are allowed to place a lien on a property if the assessments or fines are overdue: True or False
    a. True, but only if proper suit has been filed in court
    b. True, if previous collection efforts have failed
    c. False, they do not have this authority
    d. False, only Condominium Associations can do this

4. The type of insurance which protects the board members of an association from personal liability in certain situations, is known as:
    a. Flood insurance
    b. Worker's Comp insurance
    c. Property Liability insurance
    d. D&O Insurance

5. The "governing documents" of an association consists of the following items:
    a. The Declaration of Covenants, Meeting Rules and Regulations, and the ByLaws and Committee Articles
    b. The Declaration of Covenants, Articles of Incorporation, Bylaws, and the Board Rules and Regulations
    c. The Articles of Incorporation, Declaration of Rules, Florida Statutes, and the Bylaws
    d. The Bylaws, Articles of Declaration, and the Board Rules and Regulations.

6. "Transition" refers to:
    a. Rotation of board members through their terms
    b. Transfer of legal documents and archives
    c. Transfer of legal rights of a board or association member
    d. Transfer of control of an association from builder to owners

7. The Federal Housing Act (FHA) protects the following persons from discrimination:
    a. Discrimination on the basis of rental history or credit-worthiness
    b. Discrimination on the basis of handicap status
    c. Discrimination on the basis of race, color, sex, national origin, familial status, or religion
    d. Discrimination based on being a member of the board or not

8. Limited common elements cannot be separated from the unit to which it is appurtenant:
    a. True
    b. False

9. Associations, or their hired managers, should keep the following records archived for 7 years:
    a. Utility bills, invoices, receipts, and quotes from contractors
    b. Copies of bylaws, minutes, articles, and rules
    c. Copies of membership applications and denials
    d. Copies of resumes of the Directors and officers

10. The "Notice of Commencement" is used:
    a. As part of the meeting process to start the session
    b. As part of the process where a member is appointed to officer
    c. As part of the lien process when a contractor starts work
    d. As part of the developer transition process

11. Contracts for service, such as landscaping or paving, require that the lowest bid be selected:
    a. Yes, in all cases.
    b. Yes, but only if at least 3 Bids have been received.
    c. No, it is not required.
    d. No, if another bidder can perform the work in faster time.

12. A "fiduciary duty" means the following:
    a. The members of the association are obligated to pay an annual Dues fee
    b. The members of the committee budget are obligated to spend the least amount of reserves
    c. The length of time of a board member's appointment should be equal to their total membership time
    d. The members of the board are obligated to act in the best interests of the association members

13. The "Bylaws" provide:
    a. The types of meetings to be held, description of roles of officers, and voting requirements
    b. The recommended coverage levels for Worker's Comp insurance
    c. The recommended coverage levels for Property Liability insurance
    d. The establishment of the association as a non-profit organization

14. A party which maintains a Florida office and is able to be served with legal notices is referred to as:
    a. An ombudsman
    b. A director or officer
    c. A President, Treasurer or Secretary
    d. A registered agent

15. The type of insurance which would provide protection in the event of a person tripping and falling on the common grounds of the community:
    a. Flood insurance
    b. Worker's Comp insurance
    c. Property Liability insurance
    d. D&O Insurance

16. Condominiums which operate more than 2 units must pay an annual fee of:
    a. $100 Per unit
    b. $40 Per unit
    c. $20 Per Unit
    d. **$4 Per Unit**

17. "Common expenses" refers to the following:
    a. Typical items that a person needs, such as water, food, and housing
    b. **Typical items that an association needs, such as paving, landscaping, or lawn-mowing**
    c. Typical items that an attorney, CAM, or CPA might charge for
    d. Typical items which are found in the surplus reserve budget

18. A form of property ownership in which an owner owns a unit and a share of common elements which are appurtenant to the unit:
    a. **Condominium**
    b. Multi-Family Residential
    c. A Timeshare
    d. Cooperative

19. The representative body which is responsible for the administration of the association is known as:
    a. The CAM (Community Association Manager)
    b. The Budget Committee
    c. **The Board of Directors**
    d. The President of the association, Treasurer, and Secretary

20. Property that is leased or owned by the association for the use and benefit of its members is referred to as:
    a. Common grounds
    b. Easements
    c. **Association property**
    d. Community property

21. The document which designates one or more parties to vote on behalf of a condominium unit owner is known as the:
    a. Estoppel certificate
    b. Proxy card
    c. Voting Waiver form
    d. **Voting certificate**

22. To make an amendment to the Declarations, the following must occur:
    a. Board members can make this decision with a Committee recommendation
    b. Board members can make this decision without a Committee recommendation
    c. Two-Thirds of the present voting members can make this decision
    d. **After all voting and decision-making, the document must be recorded with the County**

23. The form of ownership in which legal title is vested in a corporation and the unit resident may own shares in the corporation is known as:
    a. A non-profit
    b. **A cooperative**
    c. A condominium
    d. An association

24. This was enacted by Congress in 1990 to protect those with disabilities:
    a. The FHA
    b. **The ADA**
    c. The Florida Statutes
    d. The FDA

25. Typical "limited common elements" include:
    a. Furniture, Sheds, and other fittings in the common grounds
    b. Staircases and Patio covers
    c. Playground, community pool, or tennis courts
    d. **Porches, balconies, and parking spaces**

Legal References and Statutes

Florida Statutes to be familiar with for the state CAM examination:

Florida Statutes Chart
607 - General Corporation Act **617** - Corporations Not-for-Profit **718** - Condominiums **719** - Cooperatives **720** - Homeowners Association **721** - Timeshares **723** - Mobile Homes --- **468** - Managers Licensing (CAM) **514** - Public Swimming Facilities

Final Checklist Before Taking the Exam

After you have completed the application requirements (fingerprinting, background check) and the educational component (pre-licensure course and successful completion of the course test), you are then ready to schedule the state examination at the Pearson Vue testing center.

The CAM test is administered via an electronic testing system, and will take place at the testing provider's location. The entire testing process is done via computer system. Candidates input their responses to the multiple-choice questions by entering the answer of their choice.

Exam candidates are first presented with a quick tutorial on using the computerized test system. It is very user friendly, and if there are any viewability or accessibility concerns, these can be addressed by the testing attendant. The on-screen interface features a variety of function buttons to help test-takes navigate through the test. The function buttons are located in the same position throughout each page of the examination screens. Using the function buttons, exam candidates can mark a question for review, move forward or backward one question at a time, or move to a specific question.

Test-takers can take a look at the summary display at any time during the test. The summary display shows candidates the following information:

- Number of questions answered
- Number of questions unanswered and/or skipped
- Time remaining for the examination

Steps to completing your application:

- Take your Fingerprints at an approved provider. They will transmit them electronically to Florida DBPR so you do not need to worry about sending them.
- Take the Pre-Approved 18-Hour Pre-Licensure Course (and pass the Course Exam). The course is available in both online and classroom formats. It is designed to take 18 Hours to complete. Many of the weekend courses are available in two-days, such as Saturdays 8AM-6PM and Sundays 8AM-6PM. For those who are comfortable with self-paced online learning, the web-based class experience might be a better fit for you.
- Schedule the examination appointment with a PEARSON VUE testing center.

Glossary

Appurtenant - To be included as part of the individual unit ownership. The share of ownership of the common elements in the community are said to be 'appurtenant' to the unit, meaning that it comes with the purchase of the unit. An example of an appurtenance would be an owner's access to the community pool or fitness center.

Assessment - A share of the funds required to operate the association and pay for common area expenses of maintenance and management. This bill is an item which is "assessed" against the unit owner from time to time.

Association - The owner's association is the entity which manages the common areas of the community, and is funded primarily through assessments which are levied against unit owners. Membership in the association is a condition of unit ownership, and the entity population is comprised primarily of unit owners, and elected representatives.

Board, or 'Board of Directors' - This is a group of directors or other elected officials who serve on a board of administrators and performs the oversight functions of managing the association. The board of a homeowners association is usually a one-year term and is strictly an elected, not appointed office. There is usually no paid compensation for a volunteer board member.

Committee - A group of board members and/or unit owners appointed to make recommendations to the board regarding proposed annual budgets, contract reviews, or other actions on behalf of the board.

Common elements - Items in a community which are owned jointly by the members of the association and typically are used and shared by all the residents, for example - playgrounds, community pools, entrance gates, etc. In a condominium, this is the portion of the owner's property which is not inside the unit itself.

Common expenses - These are the annual expenses incurred by the association in the daily operation of the entity and its functions, for example - costs associated with renting a Hall for a board meeting.

Common surplus - Funds from all receipts and revenues, which may exceed the costs for the common expenses. Receipts and revenues can include income from fines, assessments, or rents.

Condominium - A form of real estate ownership which includes the individual unit that is purchased, and an undivided share of the ownership of the common elements, which is considered 'appurtenant' to the unit.

Conspicuous type - Refers to marking text in a bold typeface so as to make it more visible. The type must be in CAPITAL LETTERS and no smaller than any other type on the page in which it appears.

Cooperative - A form of ownership of real estate where the owners do not actually own the property in which they live - rather, cooperative owners own shares in the corporation, which is the cooperative, which owns the property.

Declaration of condominium - The document or instrument by which the condominium is created.

Deed restrictions - This is commonly defined as the architectural and maintenance requirements that the owner must adhere to or risk incurring fines. The deed restrictions in a single-family home community are usually found in the association Declarations.

Developer - The person or entity who creates the condominium or planned unit development, and offers parcels or units for sale.

Developer's disclosure requirements - Required documentation that a developer is mandated to provide to prospective buyers of a condominium unit. These required items are different than the disclosures that a single unit owner would be providing to a buyer, and are usually quite voluminous.

Disclosure summary, or **HOA Disclosure** - A document required by the Homeowners Act which is required to be presented to prospective buyers before the execution of the sale contract.

Emergency powers - As outlined in Chapter 718 F. S, condominiums may employ emergency powers in case of damage caused by any event for which a state of emergency has been declared.

Fair Housing Act of 1968 - Also referred to as the FHA Act, this was legislation enacted in 1968 to protect consumers of the protected classes against discrimination in real estate sales and transactions.

Limited common elements - Those common elements which are reserved for the owners of a certain unit, or units, as specified in the declaration, and not available for use by all other owners.

Mobile Home - This is defined as a residential structure, transportable in one or more sections, even if the transporting action is done only once to install it in a semi-permanent placement.

Multi-Condominium, or **multicondominium** - A residential real estate development containing two or more condominiums which are operated by the same association.

Non-Profit corporation - A corporate business entity in which the dividends, surplus funds, or proceeds from revenues or investments are not split amongst the owners of the corporation, they are reinvested into the entity. The majority of homeowners associations and condominiums are chartered as Not-For-Profit corporations.

Not-For-Profit Corporations Act - Chapter 617 of the Florida Statutes, which outlines the scope of authority for a not-for-profit corporation.

Ombudsman - A government official appointed by the state Governor to investigate complaints of mis-management on the part of associations, cooperatives, or condominiums.

Parcel - A condominium unit, and all the appurtenant shares of the common elements as defined in the declarations. It is a separate unit of real estate property, and can be bought and sold to new buyers.

Protected class - A group of people with a common characteristic that are legally protected from discrimination, such as race, color, religion, handicap, etc.

Special assessments - An assessment levied against a unit owner which is not included as part of the planned annual budgeted items. Special assessments are sometimes levied in the case of an emergency repair or unplanned upgrade.

Timeshares - A form of real estate ownership in which several joint owners share the right to use the property for a specified period of time only, as part of a timesharing arrangement.

Timeshare plan - Any arrangement, plan, scheme, or similar device, other than an exchange program, whether by membership, agreement, tenancy in common, sale, lease, deed, rental agreement, license, or right-to-use agreement or by any other means, whereby a purchaser, for consideration, receives ownership rights in or a right to use accommodations, and facilities, if any, for a period of time less than a full year during any given year, but not necessarily for consecutive years.

Unit Owner - In condominiums, this is the recorded owner of legal title to a condominium unit or parcel.

Unit owner's disclosure - Chapter 718 F.S. mandates that a prospective buyer for a condominium unit is entitled, at the seller's expense, to a copy of the condominium declarations, articles of incorporation, bylaws and rules of the association.

Voting certificate - A document which indicates which one of the record title owners or a representative, is authorized to vote on behalf of a member; used in cases where there are multiple owners to a unit or parcel.

Index

Appurtenance - 43
Assessment - 78 (Table)
Association - 17
Board - 65
Budgets - 79
Committee - 75
Common elements - 29
Common expenses - 80
Common surplus - 43
Condominium - 29
Conspicuous type -
Cooperative - 29
Declaration of condominium - 29
Deed restrictions - 110
Developer - 44
Developer's disclosure requirements - 44
Disclosure summary, or HOA Disclosure - 44
Emergency powers - 68
Fair Housing Act of 1968 - 132
Limited common elements - 58
Mobile Home - 31
Multi-Condominium, or multicondominium - 133
Non-Profit corporation - 33
Not-For-Profit Corporations Act - 33
Ombudsman - 133
Parcel - 133
Protected class - 133
Special assessments - 93
Timeshares - 133
Types of communities - 29
Unit Owner - 54
Unit owner's disclosure - 44
Voting certificate - 76

References

- Florida Community Association Manager
  License Examination Candidate Information Booklet
  Published by the State of Florida, Department of Business and Professional Regulation (DBPR) - October 2019 Edition
- Robert's Rules of Order - The International Standard for Group Facilitations and Voting
  ISBN: 978-0306820205, 2019 Edition
- Florida Statutes Online Database Search - Known as the "Online Sunshine" website:
  URL: http://www.leg.state.fl.us/Statutes
- The FindLaw Searchable Law Database:
  URL: https://codes.findlaw.com/FL

Copyright © 2019. All Rights Reserved.

How to get your Florida CAM license:

1. Enroll into a pre-license course
2. Submit a cam license application
3. Get your fingerprints taken
4. Schedule a state examination

The **State of Florida Community Association Manager - Complete Study Guide** is your reliable source of information you need to know in order to pass the examination. This is the first and most-complete study guide and reference manual for candidates preparing to embark on that journey and take the State of Florida Community Association Manager (CAM) licensure examination. The test is not impossible, it is moderately challenging- and it will sufficiently test you on the knowledge and familiarity of these concepts. The goal of this textbook is to introduce these knowledge points to you in an organized fashion which is designed specifically to, and formatted in alignment with, the State-mandated curriculum for the CAM test. There is a specific learning path and personal requirements to become a CAM, most importantly, you must take the required Pre-Licensure learning class, which is available online or in-person.

www.ingramcontent.com/pod-product-compliance
Lightning Source LLC
Chambersburg PA
CBHW080458220526
45465CB00006B/2311